Loveliness

Musings on Loving Kindness and Living Justly

by Lee Anglin

Table of Contents

Dedication

With love and encouragement to our children, Bruce (passed on) and Kat, Brenda and Ronn, Brian and Lisa, Karen, Christopher and Connie; to our grandchildren: Austin, Autumn, Devin, Alexandra, Jacob, Nicolas, Luc, Evelyn and Ryan.

With deep appreciation for our friends far and near, new and old, and for our sisters- and brothers-in-faith.

With special thanksgiving for Dr. Eugene Peterson, who has done a wonderful thing writing *The Message*; especially do I thank him for multiplying a richer understanding of and daily living in Jesus, the Christ, Son of God, son of man and woman.

Lastly, while it has taken many personal years of fun, sitting at times before an empty computer screen and great hours of work to complete this compilation, my dearest friend, bride of forty-four years, soulmate and patient spouse, Carol, has been my star encourager, has rung the dinner bell and then generously waited, has deciphered and then commented on much that is here - she has offered many helping ideas, wise commentary, good suggestions and words that make meanings clearer. This has buoyed and amazed me; she is way smarter than I. While I used to think I had a fairly substantial vocabulary, hers astounds me. I cannot thank her often, or deeply enough.

+++++++++

Introduction

I cannot remember when I scribbled poem number one: it was undoubtedly something about "Roses..." and its author was, give-or-take, four-to-six years. The first painting – I was in my early thirties – a watercolor landscape, done in the basement of the Ontario Baptist Church building, Ontario, NY, near the south shore of Lake Ontario; the painting stayed in my study for a while prior to its mysterious disappearance. As a personal discipline, around 1995, I began to read and ponder the Book of Psalms (all 150 of them) and to write prayers in response to them. The prayers were mostly written across twenty years, resulting in more than 500 prayer-offerings to God. I'd planned to give the prayers a fitting name: *Yakking at God*. That may yet happen.

Having written several hundred poems in 85 years, I am including what I hope will express, if not growing and maturation as a poet, at least a real part of me – who I was and am becoming.

I am glad for this volume and offer it in an effort to care – either up close or from a distance – for you.

What this author and his friends have tried to do in this book is interpret some of what living has been during the years of playing, working, resting, suffering, enjoying and relating with other human beings and with God.

- Lee Anglin

Poems

This writer seems to have come into the world primarily a right-brained person. In childhood, I enjoyed playing both "soldiers" and with dolls; I liked arm wrestling and playing house – which was in contrast to most of my male friends who were more rootin'-tootin'-shootin' than I. Growing up in a "man's world" I learned how to be a "boy's boy" and, then, to participate in being muscular and athletic. Many of my neighborhood friends were females, rather than mostly males.

In pre-teen and teenaged years, my innermost thoughts were overwhelmingly "right-brain" images, pictures and visions. Tools and machines and cars and figuring things out held my attention much less than imagining, dreaming (in color) and drawing strange creatures and human-like beings. I was more interested in what might be than in what was. I thought in pictures and found it difficult to put rational descriptions to what I saw in both day and night visions.

Still imaginative 70 years later, and still primarily "right-brained," I continue to enjoy an active, colorful inner life. I've often said I enjoy a rich interior life. Images flourish inside that are often beautiful, sometimes odd, or dark and always colorful and frequently other-worldly. I recall being old enough to print and then to write, and to make rhymes and, growing older, to write poetic thoughts. So, if indeed my adult efforts toward being poetic may be called *poetry*, I am including some of the poems friends and other readers have commented on across thirty years of attempting to speak from within and from mind-soul.

-Lee Anglin

WE'VE MOVED ON

Before, behind, beside us
Beneath, above, within us
God's Christ calls... Come
You labored and weighed down
You sad and broken down
Come, we will make you whole
Come with me, follow me, learn of me, rest in me...
Live in me
Surprise!
I live in you
While

We... all the while
Squirm and sputter
Twist and stutter
Squeak and pull away
Sipping wine, remaining cool
We've moved on
Higher and further, up and
Speaking in concepts, fabrications, concoctions, gesticulations
Abstractions, cogitations, obfuscations, postulations we

Deny, defy, belie
We relatetalkofrelationshipfellowshipkinshipcommunion
But it's a little snug for
us

(cont'd)

Crimping our truth pursuit
We get high from ideas, erudite things to ask
Askaskaskaskwe're bent on

Personal connecting, bonding, coming near, intimacy, experiencing deeply
Within...
That's how we say it, it's our freestyle

Our dwelling place-of-preference is
High thoughts far away, stratospheric sophistries
Queries into which the old God cannot go
We've larger thoughts, deeper.........
We wind and wend and breathe profoundly
We circle 'round and back andand conjecture and puzzle darkly
And live by prepositions, adverbs and conjunctions
Stroked by circular questions and urbane hypotheses
Propositions and ponderous speculations
Stoked by long heated paragraphs and profound silences

We imagine these a better way it's our way than
The One we've moved on from.

MEMORIAL

We remember you, men, we sob
Close friends and strangers, too
We weep for your dads
And honor you, lads
It's the one thing we can do

As men of old were, we're told,
Folk cried for them as well
The lads before were killed and fell
And lay in graves drear cold

Why do we sob and linger and weep
Because you killed your brothers?
We *do* sob, friends, because *you* sleep
Because you died, as the others.

We weep because you lately sighed
Because, strong lads, you lately *died*
Because you're the lads we knew so well
The kids we'd soothed each time you fell
You're the lads we birthed and hailed
And because…
Once again,
We have failed
Once – again – we have failed

A HAT FOR BILL

The heart of the lad left
    The heart of the lad
His smile has changed
    I noticed
Where's the grin, the boyish grin
Of the child who once gaily flourished
Of the child whom once we nourished

It seems but a day… since…
He went away
As he danced and sang,
The 'star' of the gang

His eyes had laughed and
Sung and sassed but
Now they seemed to sag
Yes! Now they seemed to lag

When he said his goodbyes
We cried deep wails
Or, was it I, did only I…

      He went away with bouncing step…
      And all he said was, "Sure!" and "Yep"
      Confidence glowing…
      Freedom flowing…
      Youthful knowing…
      Wisdom growing…
      Hope abiding…
      Greatness showing

Something happened
In the heart of the lad
Is he still our beloved son
Can a soldier's hat
Bring a change like that
To our dear, our treasured one

His name was Bill...

THE CROSS

He said he would free

Us

He pledged not to leave

Us

He did deceive

Us

We aggrieve

Him

Yet we believe

Him

We receive

Him though

We don't deserve

Him

We will not preserve Him

We will follow and serve Him

Forever

RESURRECTION

My soul today is a wintry scene
Filled with wintry showers
But soon I'll dream an April dream
Splayed with Easter flowers

REAL SOUL

My soul has been
Aground a while
Acquainted with dying flowers
My heart has lived with
Frozen dreams
And drooping winter bowers

I've known dark snow
Though life is a flow
Neither down nor out
Nor dying
I was dry as a bone
My heart cold as stone
Yet always hoping and trying

With blissful love
Come from above
To share and spread forever
With thanksgiving and grace
Shalom from his face
Splashing us without our endeavor

I wonder where
The feeling went
My life of thriving and giving
No deep sorrows or rivers of tears
No frequent nightmares or recurring fears
Just the joy of striving and living

WAITING

He said he could not could not wait
His birthday driver's license and first date
First smoke high school college service job
Apartment new car travel new job
Wife children promotion education paid off
Work move up fresh start buy own want
Forty labor's fruits enjoy (it while you can)
Retiring spouse empty nest Europe at last
New job different house almost different spouse
Wait quit work appendix out
Buy afford dream of more
Retirement coming
Alwaysdoing, alwaysgoing
Years
Planning saving
Waiting fireplace sparking
Warning bypass waiting
Padded chair wheels included
Wonders...
Waited waited...
"What happened?"

PROMISE

All the light we cannot see

All the love we cannot be

All the grace we cannot live

All the peace we cannot give

All the life we cannot bring

All the joy we cannot sing

  But such as we have

  Give we thee

  Will kindness do

  For a start

SAD EYES

Clouds shrouded her

The storm shrilled fiercely

Her gaze was locked in fire

She cringing and blazing

Against the molesting

Screaming without sound

Weeping without tears

Holding the child closely

Protecting and pleading and saving

The lone Madonna knelt huddling just

Beyond the hospital door

Against no place to go

But her ancient fears

COUNSELING

We two sat facing

Each the other

In tranquilizing chairs

Fending and chirping

I ventured a hundredth of my pain

Sent don't-bother-me signals

One atop another, I broken, breaking and...

What's bugging you, sir? Please, just talk. Don't answer. Not really.

Clear, knowing eyes stared me down

I can't ask you, sir, but may I scream

Does my silence shout loudly enough

Will a pathetic shriek tell you some thing

What you don't want to know

You, nursing your precious pipe and cherry blend

If I undress, can you stand the nakedness

THE FLY

Fly at winter's end, black-winged, droopy sloth

Half-frozen slug on hesitant legs pauses jerking

Tired, looking more lost than last year

Appearing as last year's replicate

Creeping down curtain's edge

Unsure or lazy or could care less

Turning for no apparent reason

Recycling again to sleep wandering

Yes somewhere no nowhere anywhere that's where

Walking circles back again to where she

Thinks, dreams insists she started

Acquainted now with muslin dust

Bored the entire adventure

Indifferent to

The intricacies of the terrain

A joke or living a serious pathos

HAPPY JESUS

Happy strong Jesus

Rugged smiling Jesus

Happy happy Jesus

Lily white, teeth shining bright

Lord of picket fence and rambling rose

Daffodils and nosegays

Speak soothingly sweet niceness

Give tinker toys plastic soldiers

Crepe souls baptized in confetti

We're tired of Cross words

Forget the tree

Sorrow men, down men bring us low

No!

Take us to the festival

Of ostriches

SECRETS

Recognizing they were little more than whiffs of wind

Wisps that blow and play before their end

Puffs to cool fevered brows

Quaffs for refreshing tired minds and broken souls

Knowing they were made to move

To give

To trust and live

They met on a busy streetcar

Joined

And went their way

Whispering secrets

HAPPY AS A LARK

She sings her songs

Atop a telephone pole

At the road beyond the driveway

Bliss rapturing In broad daylight

Right out loud

As if she doesn't care

Shamelessly preferring the universe

To hear

Especially people and purple finches

Earthworms and tree frogs and fawns

Along with other larks but

Her prime audience

God

DON'T PRAY *HERE*

"War, I know, is hell!" said Mr. President
Sincere in voice with just
a pinch of noticeable
Trembling timbre... emotional,
"But, you must be asked to pray in the
White House
By invitation only
Like Drs. Graham and Vincent Peale
Who as every one knows are close to
God"
A *good* friend of mine as well.
To clarify the regulation says
"Anyone *caught* praying here
Without prior authorization
Will be summarily quelled then
Arrested for acts unbecoming of
Civilized persons then charged
With petty misdemeanors detrimental
To the country's national image
And decorum I might add
Don't misunderstand
My mother was a fine
Quaker woman and
Her mother, also."

GRAVE STONES

Some of them have been

Silent a hundred year up here on

The hill

Quieter than the stones

Marking and naming them

Dutch names, English, Prussian

Companions of dogwood and pine

Standing cold in the wind that

Whistles through seasoned grass

I button my Carhart against

Winter's music

Intense upon thoughts of

1809 – 1871   1821 – 1826   1811 - 1826

A BRIGHTNESS

A sun jumped up and broke

Surprised heads raised

Eyes blinked

Out in an instant

Skin became soot just like that!

Additional chemical compounds

Well known to any corner pharmacist

Piled neatly in chairs on

Beds, sidewalks and schoolyards

The cousins and moms and priests

Along with brothers, grocers, derelicts

And old ones

Weren't, they weren't and

It seemed almost ordinary

THEY WERE CALLED

They were called *Men*

Of vision since

They had monumental

Dreams

Of manly schemes

On manly themes

It was to mistake

Truth for illusion

Delusion of the mind

Caked with obtusion

A vacuous confusion

NIGHTWATCHMAN

He walks lamely

From a fall

In his life

Limping to work at

Fifty, twelve to go

Or thirteen depending

Does his job surely

Never nods his head

Although he likes the

Coffee but

He hates it

Down way down

And conjures better

Ways to spend his

Nights

IT IS COLD

The chill fills, the wet . . . Lord, it's wet!
Where'd the sun go? Rain off my
Chin shines the fingernails
Fingers turning twisting the rice straw
Making a mat... no one will buy
Here I am squatting, bent, a rotting dog
Would any come near to buy my rice-
Straw mat?
Who would come near the pale old
Woman, disfigured, gaunt,
What's she thinking to herself sitting there?
In a pile?
Not once have I had enough to
Eat my hands are claws picking at straw!
She shows no evidence of pain, just a
Look of devastation like the remains of her
Bomb-shattered hut. Listen!
Is she humming a tune? Could she...
Be singing? To herself? To God? In the
Cold and the rain? About what does a
Leper
Have to sing?

WITHOUT CEASING

Digging, scratching, fingering, squeezing
Nervous blemishes
Woman in mauve and gray
Sits in holy worship
Preoccupied with frenzy
Shredded stubs of fingernails dig
Bloodless sores embedded in scales
Hands refuse to still
Press each other and pull trying to
Make her fingers grow
The neck the cheek the nose feint under
Channeled brow and scared eyes
Stare at her feet
Somehow surviving another minute
She leaves as she came
Almost smiling as if embarrassed
Reeking terror
She gasps awake

VESTIGES

In summer
They wipe their sweat on handkerchiefs
And wrists
To tunes from
Unseen speakers
In the air
Captives to the
Company that pays
For
Defamation of character
Witting slaves
POWs
MIAs content with
$420-a-week and
Emasculation
Not knowing
Even the vestiges
Have disappeared

WAGES

It's not as though it's

A big thing – not like

Selling soul, or selling out

You know

Not in the long term, really

It seems harmless enough,

Were it not for the few

You know

Surprising shocks of

Recognition

Besides a tiny

Dollop of minor stress – you know

Ask the others, my friends

At work, they are acquainted

With what I'm saying even

Though, Joe, I believe

(cont'd)

Opined: "Somewhere in the

Caverns of my life finally

It matters that we are

Vegetating for wages."

PARK MEN

Uniform men resplendent in uniform baseball

Caps cut-off jeans solemn sneakers

With holes here there munch on baby

Carrots and sandwich meat see a

Trio of squirrels skittering up down and

Every which way until, tired out of breath

They stop, just like that, before seconds later

They off again. Thus, entertained, parked

Men down American cheese with energized

Slices of sandwich bread, automatons to

Euchre, busily waiting for Thursday's S.S

Check.

Stop.

LIFE FLIGHT

He ran after moments

And over-ran eternity

To vanish somewhere

Beyond vision or dreams

A man of minutiae

Small ideas and brittle

Plans that

Did not work

When he could stand

It no longer he ran

He ran away in the

Cold to freeze from

Life.

PAPILIO GLAUCUS

In September you're more likely to
See them along rural roads of
Vermont, Maine and New York
Maybe, some other places, too
Cars whiz by, swirling winds
Force wings to subtle moves
Of ascend and descend then calm
Again
Life waving goodbye, saluting
Having, as always, done the job
Very well... breeding for next year
Flying effortlessly smooth, adding
Serene, magnificent touches of
Beauty to wondrous earth.
They fall, not as soldiers
But lovers to be eaten by ants
Leaving behind gracious crayoned
Going-away presents: two wings
Of bright orange, deep black
Filmy shades of dark blue
And a swallow's tail to boot –
Tigers all, but with sweeter
Dispositions

AND SAT DOWN BESIDE HER

Leave off discussing with crocuses the

Winter-spring penetration of earth's

Frozen soil.

Don't commiserate with snowflakes

About the weather being cold.

Forget conversations with mice

About chemistry, or

Architectural designs.

Military stratagems never enter a

Spider's mind

She moves and dances and spins

And molds and smiles in the sunshine of

New, magic carpets.

PSALM ZERO

And he said:

"Oh! Where dwells one who cares for me?

Alas! Is there any in whose heart there sings a prayer?

Wretchedness hounds my days, every hour on the hour!

Loneliness dog-whips all my nights!

Who hears, who listens for the egregious cries and dying breaths of this

Crushed man who used to be?

I am bushed, beaten, I am ignored, forsaken!

Oh, Lord, who once loved me, take me, just take me!

I long to sleep then awake to find, I am not! I am no longer!"

Then, in the midst of the heartbroken personal catastrophe,

I heard a voice, a still, small silence sounding low

Veiled in mystery, a wordless silence from the

Depths and the voice said:

"Huh?"

LEAVES LEAVE

"Pssst!

Over here… out of the sun!

But, can we really hide from…

You know who? Are you sure?

You've done it before? Then…

Let's do it… come in here,

I'll scoot over,

Love, so you can get

Behind the leaves.

I've gotta

Say, though, we ought to get

Serious about finding some-

Thing better than flimsy, crepey

Fig leaves with which to cover

Ourselves.

I was *so* ashamed when

Creator saw us naked the first

Time. Shhhh! Creator's

Coming. Oohhh! We've had it...

This time for sure."

"Eve! Adam! Come out, come

Out, wherever you are! Oh! *there*

You are! Hello, my dearests!

I've missed you. Have you been

Hiding from me? Again? It's ok...

This time but, please, there's no

Need to hide or be afraid of me!

I've seen lots of my new friends

Nude and, believe me, you look

Healthy, wealthy and wise in my

Eyes and that's the truth. Oh! By

The Way: from now on, no more

Fig leaves for you two! How's

That for some good news!

If you're going to cover yourselves

Because you're naked and

Don't like your bodies, look!

(cont'd)

I had Michael skin a huge

Elk

So we could clothe you

Will soft

Hides do? But, listen! You *never*

Need to be ashamed. Never

Again! You hear me? Now, if

You'll, get dressed! I can't wait

To see you in your new duds!"

FOOD FOR ALL

Miraculously

God has come again

As a sunflower

To feed the Sparrows

And Chickadees, too!

LOVE IS

When in despair a soul collapses in a

Pile far back in some damp dark corner

If wearying storms howl through a mind

And ruin crashes with typhoon power

If un-named hungers gnaw in someone's

Heart beyond her ability to bring repair

Where barrenness barges in, sits down and

Makes itself at home and someone's day

Skids and jack-knifes and collides with death

Down, down to unending terrors

God is there

> As the child bitten by sewer rats
> As the derelict with no place to go
> As the starving mother in an overfed society
> As the rheumatic sleeping under city bridge
> As elbow-to-elbow emptiness trudges on rush-hour streets
> As crushed dreams keep fading with the years

God is there

Not to observe, take notes, or photograph the pain

But to put our bodies around the need

To be there with the ones who ache

To transport the child to the clinic and then to pay

Love is something like that

GOD IS LOVE

God loves the simple sheep

God loves the hunter wolves

God loves the hearts of both

God loves the falcon and hawk

God loves chickadees and doves

God loves the right and the wrong

God loves the faithful and the cynic

God loves the purposeful and the lazy

God loves the warrior and peacemaker

God loves the humble and the arrogant

God loves the sharers and the greedy bunch

God loves the spiritually alive and the legalist

God loves the truth teller and the power monger

This is a great truth and this truth matters eternally

It matters much, dear friends, for all the world it matters

Which we be

JONAH

He wasn't much to recommend
To an audience at all
Looking like something very close to
Dried seaweed, crusted brine and
Shriveled burlap half-digested, he said
To the gathered Ninevah crowd,
"SHUV!" That was it – that's all he said.
But no one *listened* or cared even a tiny bit
The roar of living was in their ears, so he repeated.
He said, "I said,
SHUV!!! And don't make me say it again!"
While they, preoccupied, played soccer and went about
Their business buying and trading and selling and playing
"Peanuckle" and another exciting new game, to wit, "Transliterate!"
No one explained or described it, but vowed
"It's way more fun than 'charades'."
It was a 'word game' and Ninevites loved 'word games'
If you ask me, which, of course, you didn't.
Finally a nineteen year-old student from the Academy stood
Before the massed congregation and,
With firm and piercing voice, chided:
"If Jonah's 'SHUV' comes to shove (the whole audience chuckled
At the student's comic word)
Jonah *loses!*
Nice fellow in many ways
But, my, the words he chooses."
All at once, looking somewhat farther along than miffed, Jonah
Shouted (in English, for heaven's sake), "REPENT!"
And the people, one and all, fell as one on their knees

(cont'd)

And faces; to a man and woman, every soul got religion
Right there and then.
That is how we heard the story, anyway – we don't know if it
Really happened that way, but,
You've got to admit, it's a
Good story!

HEAR

Hear – can you hear? Have you ears that hear. Carefully…

Hear – past the whirlwind cries and siren voices

Hear – beneath the world's confusion and human maze

Hear – somehow in the ceaseless chagrin and agonizing

Hear – among the chatter and cacophony of the embittered

Hear – mingled with the rising voices of the Black and Brown

Hear – in the fury of some and the bedlam of many of the broken

Hear – our human brothers and sisters who are named LGBTQ's

Hear – from the inwards of dead and dying warriors across the globe

Hear – amplified by the pale and wan faces of impoverished women

Hear – with and among the hungry, unschooled, hopeless children

Hear – the sighing, the weary sighing, the steady anguish and

Hear – the eternal silent word of Someone who, with great love calls:

"Adam . . . Eve . . . Where are you, my beloved? My dear children!
I'm here."

DEMOCRACY

When we have biked around the world

Wearing tasseled cowhide vests, Fu-

Man-chus, donning professional

Leather cowboy hats with Indian head-

Bands, the work of compassion will

Still be here when we return.

If, in black elevated shoes, we man-like

Stand on daises to make gutsy speeches

That make good sense, pointing clenched

Fists to he sky, shaking them forcefully,

Justice will need to be done just like

Every other day.

Scorning all the law'n'order political folk

Writing our letters to the editor by the car

Load, freedom for all will hardly be any

Closer than it was a week ago.

Will men be brothers when we make more

Laws, write stronger mandates, rules and

Restrictions? Will the nation be any less

Tainted by the KKK and the thousand

Hate groups that sliver by and hide in sheds

Loaded with Uzis and AK47s and

Things that explode and maim?

PARDON ME!

Yes, we did beat up on your heads
Put you in 'your place' and silence your prophets
Absolutely, we cut off your dreams
Then accused you of being irresponsible oafs
So? What has it gotten us?
We jailed you, lynched you, cut out your tongues
We called you accursed, we being very religious
We burned down your dwellings and from the
Bible we proved your blackness was punishment
We recoiled in disgust as you acclaimed Black
Beautiful and always wrote you out of our history
Books. We escorted you, friendly and all, out of
Our temples of holy worship, especially as you
Became 'smart'. We called you "N" (the "N" word)
And Nigra and Darkie and Colored and Spade,
Each being razors in your souls. We said you
Could come to our back doors if you had business
With us – big hearted as we were (and still are).
You were often permitted to drink from our farm
Wells (using a different dipper, of course); we've
Always been generous that way. We educated
You because the law said we must, just not in
Our public schools, k-college. We put you in
Your *own* schools and furnished them and
Educated you by default and, afterward, we
Said your intelligence was inferior, as we said
You, also, were. Pardon me, but it seems a
Pertinent question to ask: What has it all gotten
Us? We enslaved you, then, with emancipation,
We excluded and belittled you. We ravished your

Sweet daughters, then called them sluts and
Whores. We did this with impunity and went on
To hang your sons high for the clear, brutal
Crimes of glancing with greedy eyes at our
Darling little girls. We emasculated your men,
Then said they were inferior – except, we
Refused to admit although we knew, they were
In ways superior. We raped your women, then
Called our offspring half-breeds who couldn't
Date our own. We drafted your young men a
Dime a dozen to gain warriors for democracy
And refused to let black and white fight the
"Enemy" side-by-side. To protect our society
We imprisoned your teens for stealing a
Five-and-dime lollipop and kept them there
Multiple years – even as our young racists flew
Free as birds from the court house. So, what
Has our civility gotten us? How have we made
Human progress these later years? We
Degraded, berated, flogged and mutilated you
We castrated, skinned, drowned and beat you
And called you "Jig"! No, I cannot argue with
Your anger that remains, although I would
There were long-term reasons now for it not
To be. I will not blame you for raised voices
Or fiery eyes. To deny your right to defend
Yourself is not in me now. Choking out, "Oh,
Please wait a little longer" sticks in my
Throat and stays there. Be militant you
Black sons and daughters of the Creator.
But, pray, refuse to be as we have been;

(cont'd)

Be not as blind or stupid even as we know,
Unless something redeeming happens to
Our visionless souls, we'll try to go on
Enslaving while hope, immortal, will perish
From this tattered land.

HE SAID

He said he would free

Us

He pledged to relieve

Us

Did he deceive us

Should we believe

Him

Can we trust

Him

Or only grieve

Him

DUSK

I sat beneath fading hues of a summer's day,
Lazily, thoughts and eyes wandering, wondering
Body at rest, nothing distressed
It was the total ease of early evening
Willowy breezes stirred and stroked and soothed
Every part and hair and limb when,
At once, all universe broke loose and
Spilled over me. It was daunting and arousing
Above, before, around, beneath me
It was an ordered wildness
Gulls, rolling stones, pine branches, song
Birds crowding in as
Sunshine paved the lake with roads of
Shimmering flame, color was everywhere and
Shadows fled under moving clouds of metallic
Blues, the vault of heaven a silvered gray,
Ribboned with light. Terns in syncopated
Flight raced eastward toward quickening
Night while, as if hurrying to get in a few last
Swoops before dark, swallows, like balsa-wood
Planes of children, dove straight out and down,
Touching water, pulling up just in time
To glide and swoop and veer triumphantly
Left and right, obviously on maneuvers.
The softening day caught my breath as
Creation, more gossamer than lace
Danced and choired in diapason
To the tender, steady rhythm of
Lapping waves against the shore.

THE CARS

How little and small we know each other

As we pass by on the other side

Indifferent to stopping and staying a while

Aliens even to ourselves

Without intending it and with faces smiling

We've become unwitting friends to icy

Distances carefully kept and

Though the empty spaces chill us

Only a few reach across the continents

To touch

TO MY LOVE

Her softness lingers a while

And smiling eyes stay briefly to remind me

That we are more than one

She with the voice of deep pools

Below the rapids

Holds on to my hand

To reveal a dearness

MAN-CHILD

Spread-eagle, he

All three feet of him

In naked glory

Prancing in the sand

Jumping in the shallows

Awesome before the dancing sea

"Come, let us sing and play"

His hands and voice address the day.

"Yes, let us commune and enjoy, I

The sea, you the boy!" Then

Peeing salt-to-salt with resolution

"Please allow my contribution!"

MR. THAMNOPHIS

Jumping with pointed sticks

Excited teasing and giggles

Poking fun, such fun

Making tiny harmless holes

Four boys bring misery

Except they don't know

A garter snake from some

Fancied hideous monster or

Imagined venomous viper

Belly-down on the ground

Its treacherous tongue and shiny eyes

Pointed at them

In September's chill it was

Flip, pick, jab and thrust

Until growing weary

They leave three inches of tail

Wriggling spastically in the dust and

Fading sun

After a while all is still

I DON'T FEAR GOD

I do not fear the One God, the Beautiful, the Only
I am not afraid of the Mysterious, Living-universe Maker
I tremble, yes: for Ecstasy and the Joyful Presence of
        the Other
        the wholly Holy Other

It is not wearying to be a child of Grace or Kindness
Our wondrous Teacher is the One who made us –
        not we, ourselves
        oh, no, not we, ourselves!

There is no self-degrading in praising "The mighty One;
God the Lord who speaks and summons the earth…"
        not in the least
        praise is of heart and soul

I am not embarrassed that God is God and I am not
Thrilled am I simply to be a friend, a son,
        a novice follower
        a God-imaged learner

Indeed, God Eternal Friend is more by far
Than I am friend to God, offering humbled truth
I remain shameless and unafraid… above all
        For God is towering, glorious
        Empowering Love.

MRS. MOORS

Mrs. Moors cut some roses, foxglove, with three pink peonies

Designing, forming the trio carefully

Symmetrically in the proper vase and set her admirable

Rainbow assortment in symphonic symbiotic balance

Arranged studiously on the proper window sill

For her bridge party for eight at eight

And stood back admiringly enrapt

And sighed her aesthetic approval

A horticultural delight

Eight days after Mrs. Moors' maid return while cleaning

Wrapped the progressively rancid once admirable

Trophy, including slimed-stemmed roses, foxglove etcetera

In last Wednesday's newspaper and so

That was that, somehow a degrading finale

To startling, ravishing beauty

Lost in want ads, sports page and obituaries

Like it never was a lofty thing

HELL NO

Hell *is* – not will be – a nomadic invisible

Parasitic nonexistent virus sucking at us

Hitching rides transcontinentally to MS, AL, TX

Transchronologically septic, portable, exchangeable

Convertible, equitable, inscrutable

Nibbling at aortas in the dark

Incising medullas each twenty-four

Snipping skeletal sinews and tendons

Hell is socked-in midnights of shame

Sweaty high noons of agony, unbroken

Twilight creatures slipping in unseen

Hell is burned-out leprosy, not gone

Hell is reality neither real nor unreal

Hell is when love begins to shrink, shrivel, shiver, then quit

A void unavoided

Hell is there or here

This side of, not beyond six-feet under

GIMME

Gimme gimme stuff gimme laughs gimme time gimme whatcha got

Gimme just enough gimme enough gimme never enough

Gimme green gimme bread gimme thanks gimme gimme whatcha got

Gimme always needing more gimme something other than I ask for

Gimme things gimme chills gimme thrills still

Don't gimme no squared, side-handled rectangular box

Gimme what can keep me going

Gimme a better not a bitter potion

Gimme painkillers gimme guns gimme a mountain to look down from

       This hellish hangover life

       This forever smell of dead

       Always wanting always more

       And different from what I ask for

       Gimme gimme gimme whatcha got

PRIME TIME

A mist of years encumbers me a

Dryness scuttles 'cross 30,295 brittle pages

Underlined notations become crumbs on the linoleum

Something heavy crawls, pushes to surface from puberty

He infertile now as old-age wombs, once proudly fecund and homey

An invisible dead-weight bends his ancient body

    As he leans or stands there… waiting

Recalling a garden snake's belly distended by a still-jumping frog

A flycatcher, snacking on tiny delicacies, swooping out then back

Prying a bb from a girlbuddy's quad

Slamming first pitch well beyond centerfield fence

Playing horseshoes with my idol, named dad

Incongruous thoughts for someone

Well past prime or

Maybe not

THE LONELY

We have seen it, though it hides, a darkness
We have known it, masked on brows deep-furrowed
We have felt its claw cutting, tearing, shredding
We have bemoaned it, breeding gloom in a thousand hearts
We have watched it dictate
- like it belongs and rules
- as if it were owner
- wheeling as if it were king
We have run from, hated, shunned its dangerous slash
- laying down streams of sadness
- draped on bowing shoulders
- glazing non seeing eyes
- squeezing life out like a light gone
We have witnessed it whip-lash hope
We have heard it crash head-on 'gainst vital faith
We have cringed while it sucked meaning out of youth
- and fled from its icy cold
- and pulled away from its forlorn stare
- and hid from its freezing grasp
We have heard it whimper, sigh and
- cry in the bathroom
- weep in the bedroom
- sob in the den all the night through
We know it well
We know it very well
We know it exceeding well... and beyond
blasphemous loneliness

SENTIMENTALITY

Last night I cried in my sleep, cried myself to sleep
I cried for the world (and my kin and myself):
A white man, vain, walking by staring at his self in the store window
A young man, palsied, struggling to stay vertical on the sidewalk
The of-color man, sitting on the town park bench, cannot get a job
A child whimpering… apparently preferring to whimper
The white woman, perhaps a prodigal, painted and dressed as the Rainbow
The black male, like a pretzel bent by the weight of limping years
The gentleman sitting, standing, neck twisting, he quietly snorting
                    ashamed and carrying on while his fingers will not
                              answer his brain, or vice versa
A mass of flesh being "sold" on a trinket (looks like a penny clock)
The dusty, yes, dirty old lady selling scarves at bargain prices
A teenager's quick hands playing tag with the female's parts
A gasping brute in Blue's Pool Parlor, bearing vacant eyes
Two guys bantering loudly, perhaps arguing politics, obvious mates
Middle-ager women in the soda shop conversing over tea about
                              Who
                              What
                              When
                              Where
                              Why?
                    I ask myself
                    Out of the blue
                    For no apparent reason
Are we sad humanity, staring at thoughts of nations preparing for war
Are we folk, gaping at the rising dread of nations annihilating nations
Are we a world sliding into nighttimes darker than total blindness
Then I went home, combed, brushed, pajamed, lingered and then slept

EX-COMMUNICATION

neither listening to their feeling

        nor hearing their listening

modifying their questions

        to suit our own answers

convinced apparently that

        only in the making of words

        may one communicate

the tragic catholicity

MAKING OR BREAKING

Please

Ebony warriors, listen, for somebody's sake

Even if you be sick-unto-death of patience

Waiting for false, faked, fading promises to appear

There the dream is, between the cracks

Of the bleeding battlegrounds of civilization and sanity

There – in the spittle behind you – do you see it still, or at all

Did you lose it, or forget it, or discard it mental eons past

Did it lose you in the cinders of forgotten oaths

Was it taken by the powers, then angrily thrown back

Answers matter, if not for them, then for you

I, myself, fear the dream is a has-been that has been burst

I sensed a moment ago, or less, you dropped it

As one pinches then finger-flips a gum wrapper

Behind you to the sidewalk

Secretly, uncomfortably, a slight embarrassment

In case you care, somebody noticed and cared

HE USED TO DREAM DREAMS

Once he dreamed dreams remembering the details

Then the dreaming-dreams-and-remembering times went away

Except, maybe, once and occasionally he imagines

    Echoes and shadows and incoherent faces

    From somewhere bits of dullness and images

He climbs, loads, descends, unloads, climbs, loads, falls, stands

Drinks beer Friday, Saturday, Sunday

Often Monday

He is despoiled some but, somehow, still alive and

Warming more than once to the miracle of sunrises of sorts

Learning new for the first time what once he learned

    Living is not the absence of dying

    Dying is the absence of living

A HEALTHY ILLNESS

He carries a lesion inside somewhere, a heavy load

For a man to bear

Vitality, a leaky cup, drains

Nerves strained

His name, Without-a-Future, is besot

But he smiles a lot

Knowing something we do not

Forces us to wonder

If his hope has gone asunder

Although they are few who die

Smiling

I've seen one or two gently fly away

Abiding

In tenderness

DISQUIET

How disquieting he was . . . did you feel it, too?
What was he wearing . . . looked like a robe
A bit bloodied, hanging, a dirty mess
I thought he should have asked for something
He appeared to have nothing
He could have begged, for a hand-out
I'd have given him money, at least
He should have said something, anything at all
It's a helpless feeling, with somebody just staring at you
We felt sorry, all of us, for him, I know I did
Especially, I think, because he wasn't that old
Why wasn't he at his job?
Maybe he doesn't have one
Was he just trying to make us feel bad
Standing there, his hands behind his back, looking
Seriously at us . . . Heh! I'm telling you, I felt funny
Was he pulling our leg or joking or what
I thought he was listening to us, even though we didn't speak
Could he have been drunk . . . he didn't look it
Maybe he's not 'all there,' if you know what I mean
So here's this young guy in his mad thirties
Down on his luck
Should we have ignored him
I couldn't . . . do you think he was in pain
I saw red stain on his robe and a mean cut on each arm
With what would that have to do?

THEY WERE EIGHTY, IF THEY WERE A DAY

If they were a day, they were eighty at… least

Ambling their way holding hands, say

Were they propping each other up?

Shuffling some, wobbling a little, leaning left and right

A young woman, passing, smiled at them

Her eyes opening slightly wider

Then looking back to confirm her first admiring glance

As the silent elder pair

On their slow meander

Almost like waiting for the world to move under them

Together and something more

No need to talk of relationship

Seeing was knowing grace and union still live

The two disappeared shoulder-to-shoulder

Through the door of the village coffee shop

STRONG DEEP INSIDE

Our hearts are strong as we begin

Our arms muscular

Living beckons

We will be free, blissfully pulsing the eternal song

We will be responsible and faithful and attuned

So let us climb never over others and

Put no poison in our breasts

No web of traps around our hearts

Let none silence our stirrings and movements

Or our headlong quest to be borne daily fresh

We have something to give and joyfully spend

As we stand and bow at this place

Thanking each the other for being

For taking the other's hands

Mine in hers, hers in mine

Given with blissful abandon

LEGACY

We met down

A roadway

Toasted thenceforth

To that day

A thousand years

Hence

Who will know

Besides some

Long forgotten

Dust

On other

Travelers' shoes?

A GOOD MARRIAGE

We had planned to be happy

To be the rest of each other to take

The good and the harsh equally together

We determined to work at

Providing pleasure, to discipline our selfishness

And give our minds over to loving well

We pledged to provide

Instead of demand

To reach expecting only what came back

To us, nothing more

We had wanted happiness

Never, however

Could we have expected

The sun to shine

Almost

Every day

FRIEND

Friend…

    I do not need your support

    I desire your love

Friend…

    No yearning have I for your charity

    I expect your heart

Friend…

    I seek not your wise counsel

    I want a fellow traveler

Friend…

    I ask not for your leftovers

    I ask for you

Signed: Yeshua

Unconditionally

SPIRIT RULERSHIP

There's an unquenchable thirsting in the mind
There's an inextinguishable burning in the soul
Something restless, vibrating, oscillating, penetrating
His spirit trembles and stretches
Forward, upward, outward like
An infant, 260 days in the womb
Unable to speak, yet knowing
Incapable of reason, yet assured
Stammering, stuttering, waiting, sputtering
But no longer silent
His faith is not producing... it is out-of-step, yet
Somehow, out of the shards of his heart
      An instrument of peace is being fashioned
Somehow, from the sweepings and scrapings of living
      A holy sanctuary is being built
What he sees in himself as papier-mâché
      Is the very fabric of eternity
Blessed is he who knows his spiritual impoverishment
The rulership of the Spirit of Christ dwells in him

HOW TO TELL YOU

I do not know how to tell you

I do not have the words to use

Words cannot express what cannot be spoken

To describe it is impossible – like describing

A boy or little girl or God

I can only say something and hope

The beating of unseen wings will be, if faintly, heard

My best is to fumble out subject and verb

> And put an exclamation point at the end and then
> Maybe the quiet glory will get through to you

That is all I can do, but

Perhaps it is enough

Perhaps his coming will say

More than ever you could expect

Were you to expect the most…

Jesus, the Christ, is coming tonight

CHRISTMAS POEM

Who could, but he, from out the grave come

Wet grave . . . natal home

Shepherd's cave . . . God's dome

Pale female . . . hale male

Brave twosome

Future gruesome

The child a whimpering Jew

From the God of the few

How could God come from a womb

Is such a God bound for a tomb

MAKE HAY

In crammed elevators and lifts and airports
In alive bodies on athletic fields and picnics
In school rooms and homerooms and corridors
In Easter Christians gathering and twelve-step meetings
In villages by the hundred score
In housing projects designed for the 'masses'
In speeding commuter trains and rush-hour taxis
In "Go-Go" palaces where bottoms and flying limbs touch
In song-filled bars on Saturday night and Fridays-after work
In hospitals, factories and industrial complexes
In store fronts and cathedrals and shacks
In living rooms and back rooms and safe rooms and tearooms
In bedlams, ghettos, prisons and jails
In theatres, night clubs and play houses

> There is a living being hammered out
> There are potentials to be uncovered
> There is celebrating to be enjoined
> There are facts to be faced
> There is faith to be lived
> There is joy to be experienced
> There is peace to be shared
> There is love to be known
> There is God
> Great day in the morning! There is God!
> Let us, then, on with it while it is yet day!

SHADOWS

When specters of pain engulf your soul
If phantoms of sorrow break down your heart
Were impenetrable fogs of loss to permeate your days
Remember
When the daily grind of fatigue beats you 'til you're raw
When harbingers of illness suck away your years
If omens of fear nibble all the night through
Remember
These are nothing more than the passing shadows of
Eternal Reality, upon whom you may depend
Reality who can bear your deepest pain
Truth who will supply your every need
Faith who can crown all your years with hope
And ignite your love again
This is the Mystery:

      Longer than your longings

      Stronger than your distress

      Brighter than your darkest sorrows

      Lovelier than your fondest dreams

"Come unto me all you who labor and are heavy laden…
      and I will give you rest"

                     - Jesus

A WOMAN

Her body, her life speak from depths and resourcefulness
    Of love and work and children and burdens
She breathes evenly, or heavily, with quickened expectation
    But, mostly, she breathes deeply and thankfully
She wonders, standing in the twilight door, where her children are
    And keeps watchful vigil with the clock
Her hands have soothed and scolded and waved goodbye
    And wrung and waited patiently
She is not easily discouraged, although sometimes weary
    With smile wrinkles at the corners of her eyes and mouth
Young men turn to her for self-awareness, meaning, for passion
    Correction, comfort and direction
She cuts away presumptions, braggadocio and trivia
    Hypocrisies, straw-castles, shoddy words
    Inane flourishes and stupidities of her sons and men
She walks softly on the land, trusting the future
    And longingly seeks the joyful day
She is often whipped, but not beaten
She may be overcome, but will not submit to death
She knows setbacks, but refuses to be deterred
She may be scorned, but keeps moving forward
Is she soft? Intimidated? Compromised? Beaten?
Never
Is she wise, sturdy, balanced, loving?
Ever
Such is the soul of the woman we love
She is on the move, giving herself for the undeserving
Some call her "prostitute," gnash their teeth at her equilibrium
But she, preferring no man, calls to her
Children of dust and clay
She is Freedom . . . Now and forever

WAYS OF THE ETERNAL

Sometimes winds move softly in and among the trees
        As if to soothe them
Sometimes the breeze caresses leaves with tenderness
        Like a mother fussing over her priceless month-old
Sometimes snow and rain and cold and hot
        Are the winds' obedient servants
Sometimes pine and poplar bow to her in-rush
        To rise again with her hushed pause
Sometimes the wind moans and hovers over seas and earth
        Mimicked by parent over child
        Child over parent
Clouds and limbs resist not its directions
Seeds go free transported by its ebb-and-flow
        To who-knows-where
Melodies and fragrances, dust and dying breaths get
        Borne on it wings
Who knows from where the winds come
        Or to where the winds go
        Who knows the winds?
The ways of the Eternal
        Are robed in mystery
        And filled with surprise

CREATIO EX NIHILO

A rib, some mud and an apple

Cain's spouse, 969 years for Methuselah

A flood, the rainbow sign and the fire next time

Babel's tower and Babel's babble

Jacob's ladder, brothers-of-Joseph caper

Moses' bush, the plagues and water sports

Manna, Sinai, Fracking around Jericho

A Samson haircut and Jonah's calamitous trip to Spain

And Job's last days

Proverbs 22:1

Daniel the Great Lion Tamer

Tragic homelessness in Assyria, or not

Virgin Birth, miracles, transfiguration, the "keys"

He, buried and resurrected

And, Oh! Shadrach, Meshach and Abednego

All ye religious, come and feast upon the morsels

With such ambrosia even the most demanding gourmet will salivate

AN OFFERING

What can I offer
I'm not six years old
Others call me poor
Talk about my clothes
And say I need a bath and push me out
What can I bring
I don't have a lot . . . maybe
Mushrooms in spring
Dandelions in summer
Clean snow come wintertime . . .
Probably not...
How about my cut-out picture of the dog
I'd love to have, or else
Some squeezed honeysuckle flowers, Oh!
I know!
I'll tie some cans together on a string
I've seen decorated cars driving by
With people blowing horns and laughing
But . . . there you are
I don't have a car

COLDNESS

He's hated his last seven winters

In Toledo and Chicago and Helena

And Detroit and Rochester NY

Winter is the cold-bloodied enemy of

His bones, who don't comprehend it

Neither do his joints, no

They're in constant centuries of pain

Since his roots are in Atlanta

All in all, however, his Enemy isn't winters

But an arctic heart

Frozen face

Cold hands

And dreams, like broken icicles

Buried in the snow

THE PAST

I curse it often

My past, what was, never far away

I yearn: let it go, or, preferably, die

Perhaps it can do neither

Gliding or stumbling along a low road

Bearing a handful of half-remembered

Reflections from . . . from . . .

I've had glimpses of a promise

Fleeting images

Or passing fancies

That slip away more quickly than they came

Hope – there's always hope (is what 'they' say)

And maybe that's enough

Just an occasional, temporary reflection

Of something good

Again, maybe there's more

THE GULL

It didn't see me, the sea
Gull just flashed overhead
I imagine it has seen many like me
From a seagull's perspective, that is
It has seen a lot, no doubt
      surfers, lovers, sunbathers, flying fishes
      and ships at sea
But it didn't see me, I think and
I wondered
      what does a seagull do about dirty air
      scream some, maybe, or endure
Seagulls have no hands, or Visine to get
The red out, so, I concluded
      seagulls are not free
      not "as a bird," as the saying goes
But one did soar by, having wings
It will fly again, and land, and walk, and eat·
And procreate, perhaps, and fly again
And die
I will, too
Die, that is
But my heart will not be in it
Because I want to fly
Never mind the "friendly skies" or
The "going great"
Just fly, or laugh
And really mean it
Which are almost the same, somehow

CONFRONTATION

You're a smooth peace talker but a lousy war maker, in short
    You're a faker
You speak much of equality while you annul the rights of others,
    Your brothers
Your brotherhood week is a hate-breeding sham
                    you're a dark American scam
You want no man, you say, to know hunger or disease
                  Your words are lies so, please!
You regularly condemn gossip and lies and slander
    But you sound like a honking gander
Your religion is a cheap and ugly oddity
      You've twisted good religion – it's only a power greedy
      commodity.

AT TIMES

Sometimes I feel that, if only I were living in Los Angeles, or Paris, or New York, I'd have a much better chance to live life fully.

Sometimes I feel that, if I were a medical doctor or college professor, I'd be one of the most happy and personally fulfilled persons on earth.

Sometimes I feel that, if I were more sophisticated and had traveled to more places in the world, I would have a greater chance to succeed.

Sometimes I feel that, to work in South America, or Africa is somehow better than working in Dallas, or Des Moines, or Durham, or Detroit.

Sometimes I feel that I will never have the time to do the good I once dreamed of doing and wanted to do for the world, but I wonder.

Sometimes I feel that some people have hurt so many other people they do not deserve to be forgiven – but, now, at 83 I see it differently.

Sometimes I feel that feelings are probably the worst realities by which to live, but I really don't want to go through life being only rational.

Sometimes I feel that God is more real than any one or any thing else on earth and, for me, I'm confident this conviction will be permanent.

Or not.

PHALSE PROFITS

They prance and pawn prophecy for petty profit

And play at 'priesthood' for popularity and praise as

The people perish, pass out, or petrify and

The preposterous pontifically plump parse pericopes from pulpit

And piddle parish prattle,

Prevaricate pablum panaceas and palaver pompous predictions

Paralyzing peace, prayer and progress

Pansy-palmed padres prepare the plundered and point

Paupers to paradise

Painting pictures of prosperity and power for

Pre-payers, post-millennials and pinchpennies...

Perfect!

CHILDHOOD GONE

I used to wonder at so many things

Standing, for one, looking at our sliding mirror

Why I didn't move, too, with the glass when

My sister opened the sliding door

Now I don't (wonder, that is)

And it bothers me some

Where did my child go

In the growing

It isn't clear, but it seems somehow

A loss

ONCOLOGY (THE STUDY OF TUMORS)

Everything inside me

Every ounce and inch and capillary of me

Says, "No! No way! Nope! It can't be!!!

This isn't happening to me!"

I'd scream if it would help.

Some times it helps a bit

I knot my fist and slam it down and spew

"Damn! Damn it!"

The jarring quiet of friends

Who were never quiet before gets to me

They're nicer than necessary, than I need

I don't know – maybe I'm the distant one

With much on my plate to do and be and live

In this brief time and

Here I am, wasting it

With thoughts of dying: will I learn to give thanks… soon enough?

SHE

She wondered, she said, if I cared

For her

And I wondered what she meant

Saharas don't know what showers are for

Deserts don't believe sunshine grows Vermillionaires

My eyes were arid a very long time

And she noticed

But, what she saw in them was

A fertile oasis

Her vision was a miracle

THE SECRET

Years ago

We spoke of loving each other

Forever

No matter what or

'Til death

And we meant every word

Scarcely imagining, never thinking

We could lose what we

Thought we had

But didn't

Although we worked hard

To keep it live

Or to keep from one another

The secret that

It never was

A TENDER SOUL

She had always been a tender girl

And her soul crashed from a bitterness

And lay there, jerking, as in death

She wept long and deep and tortuous sobs

Against her knight's indifference

And got nothing in return except

Darkness and clouds and bored sighs

She had given herself to a male who

From childhood

Had only known how

To tear up his toys

Yet somehow, someway

She remained a tender girl, a tender soul

More so, I tell you, than ever

CANDLES

Candles are not for burning

At noonday

He said to the Sun

Fretful that its awesome

Shine dimmed his own

Nevertheless he stood

Afire

Since he was a

Candle, after all

MY PARENTS

Fixed are they in this beating heart

Well-deep in the deepest part

Of me

Living inside like oaks and orchids

Still growing there, the pair

Unknown to most but

Kin to God

Progenitors of this body and soul

And these clay feet

Co-creators of this flesh and bone and mind

They rest now beneath the sod on a hilltop

Where I've walked but once

Hail! Hail! To you

And farewell!

THROUGH IT ALL

She will smile through it all

Only the fatigue in her lines will reveal

The pain

You'd have to know her to see that she's afraid

It's hardly noticeable

Most of us would be, too were we told of a sudden

Life is dearer than we thought

She doesn't want slipping away

She recoils… at the thought of it

At the hurt of dying

She is honest that way

She's incredibly human

INFREQUENT CUSTOMS

Her custom was to love us as we were

Though we didn't, or couldn't, or wouldn't

Always accept her terms . . .

We didn't know how, but

She loved us, no matter

And when she had no other way to encourage us

She'd be simply for us, on our side

Not necessarily whether we were right or wrong

I can't remember if we ever told her she was a giant

Probably not

I wish we had

If we didn't, she didn't mind

She was all the time so busy

Loving with abandon

PROMISES! PROMISES!

There were friends, too, who sat at watch with her

Toward the end

And touched her frail life

Talking gently, if somewhat awkwardly with her

Not knowing exactly what to say to someone so alone

She weighed 67 pounds and hurt all over

We were there hovering possessively

As if to protect her from the dark wings descending

We smiled at her face and eyes

To catch what seemed a single coal aglow from

Deep within

We smoothed her sheets and changed her open side

And cried

Honestly, it felt like God was away

And the only thing we had was a promise

FAIR AND UNFAIR

Life is so unfair is how we saw it

But, really now, that's how life is

It irritated us – her family and friends – some, I think

That she didn't complain

Or even to notice as we did

How, somehow, she made it seem good

She'd honored and loved living and still did, steadily

When she died it was not by forfeit or whimper

Dying had to catch her in sleep

She opened her eyes as if by surprise

She already knew the icy hands

And moved from us as she had lived . . .

Softly, carefully, fiercely

As the saying goes . . .

Getting old is inevitable

Growing up takes practice

INSTRUMENTS

We two are stringed instruments

You the violin, I a fiddle

Both carefully made

Responding to the lead violinist's strokes

Eagerly, focused

Side-by-side is where we belong

Here we shall learn new harmonies

Both day and night

And listen to and teach each other

So stay with me a while

Until the music hidden in my strings

Finds its way to yours

Which already is singing me

To life

A FLOWER NAMED 'TULIP'

Nine months she pondered how
To make her cold
Alien world better, more beautiful again
Being small among so many
Who shoved for space
She couldn't do much
It was late winter – and an awareness, a
Stirring started deep inside
And she began to push
Not against but up because
It was in her,
It was part of her to push
Moving powerfully inside and upward
No matter the cold outside
No matter the unyielding earth
No matter what
One Sun
Day she opened to the world
Declaring in the way tulips say it
'Love to you
All you my sisters and brothers!'

TOGETHER

We came together
Shyly
As newborn fawns
Breathing warmly, tentatively
In the early morning of our days
You moved soundlessly to my heart
And took up residence there
Bringing subtle songs
And healing waters inside
Flavored with sunlight
Softly, softly you touched
The edges of my life
Knowing somehow your inviting, wry smile
Would be enough to penetrate
The important parts
Changing nightmares to dreams
Illusions to new perceptions
Confusion to commitment
Virtual affection to eternal love

TO CAROL

Dear Carol,

This morning the sun woke up for us

This morning the darkness fled and the dawn sprang up for us

This morning the sky renewed its blue for us

This morning all the cardinals and finches and blackbirds and larks
        Sang for us, and the hawk soared for us

For others, too, but only by your permission.

Carol responded

Dear Lee

I love you!

Signed: Carol

CLOSE

I do not want to possess you

Though there are times I am

Possessive

Or fearful of losing you

Because I do not love myself healthfully enough

I do not want to own you

You are intended for open arms and

The freedom to be responsible

I often grasp at you, try to hold on to you

Prodded by an unsure self

Stretching to anxiety in the presence of

An awesome, beautiful soul

I do not want to smother you, or

Entrap you, or imprison you

I want to feel you close enough for a moment

And to flower you with the

Rest of my life

BLESSING, LUCKY, OR GOOD FORTUNE?

Yes, I'd say I'm lucky

Five decades together without

Dying, or taking each the other for granted

Or dreading the days, the moments

Except a few times

I know so many feelings

Too many to recall, celebrate or share

It's surprising at my age

Since I once supposed I'd be gone by now

Or, worse, that I'd be way old

I'm grateful, dear friend, to you

For it is you, partly . . . . . . *mostly*

Who keeps from perishing in me

Much that would be worn, or useless, or decayed

Had you not been and been

Around

GENTLENESS

The clouds had

Flown away and hid

While we danced and

Dried our hair with

Handkerchiefs

She laughed

As she smoothed the

Droplets from my brow

A sunbow haloed

The smiling sky

And we hailed each

Other with kisses

Dreams

And gentle whispering

SEEDS FOR OUR DAUGHTER

Soaking up her sorrow with her

Fingers

Brushing the weariness away with her

Voice

Her comfort flows

Quietly through her smile

Watering the seeds of

Tomorrow

A PLACE NOT FAR

There is a place

Not far from here

At the centers of my mind

Where visions dawn

Upon a life

Once Still Once

Lifeless

Now born anew each moment

From a single touch

Of the soul

By healing hands

And transforming laughter

And excellent embrace

WALKING WITH THE OTHER

I will walk with you

Trying never to insist that you

Be in step with me

For ego's sake

I will offer a hand to hold, a

Smile to enjoy and

Craziness

And purple scotch tweed tigers

Understanding that your gifts

Run deeper

And being happy about it

I will love you through winters, springs and

Other times, as well

Leaving you free to love

As you love, unencumbered

With a long, deep quality of

Eagerness

SUN

Clearly

She knows the

Sunglow has befriended her

Whose face shines with ancient suns-down

And childhood's suns-up

Her rising brings

Sunshine

To darkened places

In the soul

Sun-showers

To arid spaces

In many lives

Sunflowers

And God graces

To the earth

KNOWING

I'd like to know you, child-sister

Until we know each other well

Which is to say, forever

There being so much to discern

In so brief a time, since we have

Just fifty years or more

Allow me first to become acquainted with

Your eyes

Already they have taught me how to stammer

And my mouth to dry

Already I have seen in them images of beauty

Enhanced by sorrow

Pain that breeds tenderness

Compassion reaching out

An expressive radiance of anticipation and

The sunburst of love, along with joy deeply flowing

Is there a single word for "flowering, delicious eyes"?

LITTLE GIRL

What if

Thirty inches of little girl

At play with salty earth

Accepting ocean as a

Mother long forgotten and then remembered

Bending straight-legged from the waist to gaze

In awesome crusted seashells

Exploring sand castles and building

Giant hangars for magic frogs

Smiling with the waves and

Spread-eagle toward the world's expanse

Just about says it all?

HUMAN CELLS

Smiles play across her face

As if

Her very cells are happy, she

Acquainted with grief and

Harm's ways

Belongs to a family of

Sunflowers

Whose character is

Illustrious throughout

The land and all creation

Fathered by diamonds

Borne upon the vast northern

Lights

WORDLESS PASSION

Is it possible

To feel you kiss me with your eyes

And remember imprints of caresses

Given with a glance

We speak unmistakably caring things

Uttering not a word

Or needing to

It is impossible that two so different

Stand in a rare bright union of

Daisies and rainbows and hurt

Something, we know not what or how

May happen to the spaces between us

To make them unimportant

Except to cherish since

They connect, not separate

And enhance the moments of our being

Together

UNTIL

A pitcher of

Tarnished silver

Sat in the corner

Empty and blemished

And lonely, having forgotten

Not knowing what it was missing

Until

Some wildflowers

Came with gifts and

Visions of elegance and charm

And a touch of subtlety

It was then that an old silver pot

Stood up straight again

THE CHRIST

As a breeze to the still deep silent woods

You came

The leaves stirred with

Magic, long limbs curved as arms

In slow motion ashes and willows moved

Dancing for joy to your music

Crickets, swallows, tree frogs and owls trilled

New songs while, for a long time before,

In that voiceless woods

They had thought themselves

Mute

You came and the great forest

Played and sang once more

TO GOD

You remind me of

Sunlight

Chasing fog and clouds

Warming winter's sky

You remind me of

Sunlight

Dancing on lakes

Flowing through fields of grain

Lighting earth, shining on

Forest flowers

Where no one walks

But the grateful

You remind me of Sunlight

At dusk time, right after a summer rain

Or is it sunlight that

Reminds me of

You?

CHILDREN'S STORIES

I looked and peered

But they had gone

Everyone of them

The daisies of the fields

The spacious green and beautiful

Doves, too, in my dream had flown away

I thought, perhaps, to visit the prince of peace

Waiting, I finally caught the faintest fragrance

The glimpse of one airborne creature borne by a

Breeze, disappearing at the horizon

Following after a distance in time I found the

Daisies

In your hair

The doves, too, were there, making sweet sounds

Sitting very still, dozens of them resting on

Children's heads and around your feet

As you told them stories

That made them giggle and laugh out loud

And stretch their wings excitedly

And open their petals even wider to the sun

BE WHO YOU ARE

Only be yourself today

Someone will come

Closer to the love of the

Holy One if you are

Be yourself and shine,

My dear

That sons and daughters of

Sons and daughters may

Bliss and enjoy

We flower with many seasons

Unfold refracting blossoms and

Await fresh blizzards of

Yellows, pinks, blues and browns

AT HOME

That morning

About eleven

Someone brushed against my

Soul

Her quick glance felt like forever

The visual embrace came swiftly

Truthfully, so purely

It touched my being with kindness and we

Found concord in our breathing

Our hearts trembling, rejoicing, singing

So simply we

Felt and

Were and

Remain

Deeply at home

WELFARE

I just don't know what
We're going to do with you
Your whole pathetic story is far out of
Hand
If you want my opinion
(You probably don't)
Don't we buy your food for you?
You don't thank us
The county pays your rent
You're not grateful
It would seem the least you could do is
Clean up the place once in
A while
I know how your medical bills are paid
It's a free ride, if you ask me
(You didn't)
My taxes go up and up and up
And you have the gall to
Complain!
Yes! I know they
Sterilized your daughters
And they'll be on
Welfare, too, just like you
We both know that, don't we?
What can I say, Yolanna, but,
"Get a job!"

THE CHILD

I saw a house a week or so ago with
This ugly dirt yard, a lot of dirty dirt and
Lots of balled-up fast-food bags,
Broken toys, mangled old clothes and
Waterlogged mags, mostly shiny pieces
Of green or brown glass strewn around
The house was broken, too, with rusty
Bent corrugated tin siding and windows
Covered with cardboard and torn plastic
That flapped; a school desk – the kind
With an inkwell, iron legs and a raise-up
Top – aged outside the door; it was an
Eyesore, cracked and weathered, with
Initials carved long ago near the pencil
Holder. For some reason the house and
Yard and broken desk stick to my mind
The four-year-old sticks harder
She was standing there looking at me.
I thought, she's thinking thoughts.

THE LADIES

Three elder women: two white, one black
Chalk-and-red canes clicking, out of sync
Jabbing the sidewalk, hardly audible tapping
Traipsing across the busy intersection, it was
A sure thing they knew the way by heart
Where cars stop and wait, even after the
Lights change, rooting for them to make
That curb! "Come on, now! Step up . . .
Now! 'Atta girl!" Anxious, dramatic husbands
And wives bet on the three running
The traveled obstacle course, experienced
Soldiers, practically sure-footed, only a single
Minor skirmish with a department store column
Taken in stride as veterans will it's part of
Living. It could be, I'm sure, hell being with-
Out eyesight or vision – getting from side-
Walk to streetcar, or street corner to street
Corner; it was odd to me: the trio didn't seem
To notice at all – but, it has to be real hell
To walk around dead.

LOVE CAME

At just the right moment

At precisely the needed hour

When the world waited

Hushed and still

And could wait no longer

Love came

Every day since that day

The world has gotten up

Brighter.

IT MAY BE INSTINCT

Although they don't seem to

Know why – any way they don't

Tell us – geese fly north, then

South, then back again. It may

Be second nature to them now

. . . like smiling, like the smile

She smiles and laughs for no

Good reason right out loud, it

Is her way in life and being and

Living with miles to go and each

Person to love and care for, she

Welcomes each moment and day,

Each friend and stranger (to her

There are no strangers) she's

Always inviting folk in from the

Cold, calloused, indifferent world.

RAIN

The world was new this morning

In freshness and blue

And many shades of green

And flying things that sang

Good songs for the ear

They (and we) were happy for the

Freshening, long summer rains in the night

That soothed the parchedness away

Storms of good cheer

LOVE'S COLORS

He'd never met love's colors

Face to face

Red and orange and yellow

Green, blue and indigo

Violet, or ever looked;

Easily bored he didn't like

To search. Myopic, he was

Fearful of colors, especially

ROYGBIV

Suspicious and discomforted

His color blindness almost

Killed him until someone

With seeing eyes embraced

Him – now they the two of

Them are a rainbow

CROSSING

We will cross together

Sensitive to our weakness

You to my fear of deep waters

I to your fear of the dark

We in this moment shall be

The rest of each other

I will be the oarsman

You will guide the bark

The sea could crest over us

Night will surely encompass us

Nothing will overwhelm us

A MEADOW

Swaying, moving around in circles

Inclining then standing straight and tall

Oscillating, moving this way and that

Oodles and passels of timeless flowers

Bow, then teeter and swing amidst the

Whispering winds as earth weaves a

Web of grace dedicated to dreamers

It's a miraculous thing to be or live in a

Meadow

A FANTASY

Once upon

A summer breeze

They came to rest

One quietly graceful

Beautifully strong

In soft blues and gentle whites

The other sun bronzed

A piece missing from its wing

Flying a little sideways

It is not common

But they liked each other

And made their home in a morning glory

WE

We were planted in fertile soil
Side-by-side
And we've used this brief moment of years
For living
Watered by the streams of a refreshing love.

We've gotten in each other's light
From time-to-time
And our branches, meant for caressing
In the wind,
Have hit and chafed and worn sometimes, instead.

We shall grow on, urging patience,
Since being trees isn't easy.
And we'll hope for fruitfulness
And our limbs will intermingle.
Oh, may our roots entwine deeply
And take their strength from the same Source.

And let the butterflies and bird and squirrels
Play among our leaves
And hide, if need be, in our shade from the
Heat of the day.
And let's welcome children when they climb
To make their marks on us
And to sing their songs of joy.

BIRTHING

She was thirty and

It was a first for her, as it had been

For others almost for ever

And she didn't know what would happen

Or what to expect (she'd been coached but

Couldn't comprehend, not exactly).

Or how it would be

Or what she'd do, or feel, or how she'd act

But she knew . . . she knew somewhere

Miles and eons deep inside

It would be in time, the

Ripening fullness

When creation would bond

With her welcoming fruitful spirit then she

Would yield her insistent holy

Treasure

HON'

Hon'

You've done

Untolled repair

To my heart

Thanks, Lee

BOSS AT THE OFFICE

Office lady used by day

You've painted a tight face between rounds

And masked pale lips for another go as

Something dour, or sad holds your eyes

Beyond the plaster smiles

Did you rum away the lunch hour at

Melissa's Bar or

Was the time a time for inner weeping

Now you're back to touch your H & P or

Apple and filtered nerve conditioning

Silva-Thins:

Confidants for disenchantment and commiseration

HIS FACE

A sleep came over him

In answer to the heavy lids

Dark, almost blank eyes stared

An instant, or not, then

Disappeared in slack retreat

Or oblivion

The tiny boy drooped off the edge of

Consciousness

To the beat of hurting bones

And bloated belly . . . . .

A dark lullaby passed over his face and

He grew very still

CAGES

First verse:

Cages have a way about them

Of changing songs to chirps

Does one forget from lack of flying

That containment isn't life?

Second verse:

Moments, for some

Are an eternity

For a few

They are eternal.

FOR FUN

You perchance might sight
The night flight of the
Night mite who in
Full flight and full height
Might light right on a kite
In flight who'll start a fight
After losing a bite and
In total plight
To the delight of
The night mite
The sight of the flight
Of the night mite
Might be a fright
Sight to some mite who'd
Watched and become up tight and
Herself taken flight
But not Mighty Mite
No, not our night mite
Right?
Outa sight!

FATALISM

Two hundred billion years

Crawl beyond tomorrow's

Void

By a galaxy day

Stars blink out

Incessantly one by one

To mystify deists and spiritualists

With final

"NO!"

Then the end

Whatever that means

It will not matter

One whittle or fly's death that

We lived

GET A JOB!

They've begun to wonder some
About you
And worry a little
When you're so talented and smart
And have so much to offer
And bring to your plate
But you have no job
It's been a while
Alright they
Can understand
They've been unusually sympathetic
Because of your problem
Being a preemy and all
And the home situation two
Years ago, but
Today's another day and
It's really getting old and a long time
Your friends wonder
If something is wrong
Oh, not so much with you, they say
They don't come right out and ask
They just wonder, they *do wonder*
And if there's something they can do
To help
They say, if, after all this time
You've not gotten yourself together
Or made it yet
And you don't know either,
Well...............

IN BOXES

Dozing men on park benches extol them
Politicians, especially men, avow their fame
But the boys, they just want to come home

WW II vets wave flags, turn red around the neck for it
Industry wigs salute, smiling their way to the bank because of it
But the boys just want to come home

True patriots demonstrate against demonstrators condemning it
Coffee shop philosophers buzz with weighty debates pro and con
But the boys, they just want to come home

TV ads and electric-wire pole posters shout the manly strength of it
Through their tears parents declare the duty and American way of it
But the boys still just want to come home

Caesar says "we've never surrendered or lost one yet!"

And the Romans pant and shout and raise balled fists and cheer

But the boys just want to come on home

They will

We promise

They will

And the boys do come home

(cont'd)

In made just-for-them boxes

Now . . . now we'll call them "Men" and be so proud doing it!

SLEEPING

It was in sleep
I think
There were piles and piles of stone
Boulder-size
Stacked in tall massive heaps
To build a wall
It was a wild, forbidding picture
Rows of mountain high rocks
Miles and miles of them
But no people
And I thought there *should* be
People, a lot of them
And it came, a message came that
I alone could not move them all
The piles of stone
Or tear it down if they made the wall
Finally I said each person should
Pick up one, perhaps, or two and walk afar
Then while sleeping I came awake
I'd forgotten something
There *were* no people, not one
Inhabiting my sleep, so
I waited , , , and waited for some
And was suddenly
Awake . . . I'd been sleeping
Must be hours so, checking the
Digital chronometer, it was almost
Four and a half
Minutes

(cont'd)

Then I couldn't return to
Sleep

AN ACQUAINTANCE

Acquainted with skin

We suppose we know the soul

We cannot wait on intricacy

Or ponder the delicacy

Of each the other

We know the facts, the outs

But fumble and obfuscate the ins

Pretend to engage the mysteries

Make peace with the façades and

When on infrequent occasions

We meet the authentic and real

We look down and want very

Much to twiddle our thumbs

I call it, "eating the crumbs"

POLITICAL MERRY-GO-ROUND

Swept along on a trillion words
Rolled swiftly by seas of change
That change not, that change nil
They ride the crested waves
To an illusory shore, what's more
Where, basking in neon victory
They divide the artificial spoils
Oblivious to the scandalous horde
Of skulls and bones of bigger
Fish that cover the clutter of
Sand around them for now the
Beach is all theirs a spell a while
And will be for a time and then
The tide named discontent will
Turn again.

DREAM NUMBER TWO

Night terrors from

Icy ships

Tumbled like balsam sticks

By a watery expanse of

Sea as mouths gaped

Beneath frozen eyes

That scream but make no

Sound

Leaving echoes of the past

Stuck in the waves a wet

Chill seeped in and over

And closed on desperate

Rouged cheeks and faded

While children played

Slide down the oars

LATE AUTUMN

Red-cheeked with autumn
We raced the leaves
Across the browning yard
Pirouetting with the swirls
But little was known to us
Then about such things -
Last year the world, we
Would have thought, was
Dying for sure and we would
Have believed it had we not
Remembered way back
When actually it was Mary
Cecil who recalled, she
Having lived so many years
More (she was five and a
Half, one year more than
I). Otherwise, we would
Have been sad for the
World but this year, much
Wiser in the ways of human
Life we jumped the piles of
Crunchy golds and yellows
And reds until supper

SMALL MEN

He twangs, they strum
Small men as on guitar strings
They pluck, he picks
Quickening the speed a
Shining sweat on arms on
And chests and shoulders
Pressure racing they
Bang wildly thumping
Jumping bumping screaming
Until one after another
From E to G peasants
Lie broken in rice fields
And ditches and trenches
Twisted face-down in
Blood-mud oozing from
Unhearing ears while the
Confronting musicians having
Performed their tympanic
Gig fly away way up thirty
Thousand feet relaxing
With Camels

IF WE LIVE

If we should live forever

The hours will be too brief

And days will be too short

But, given the years and

Times we have shall we

Try to learn each other

Oak and willow . . .

Hawk and swallow?

Tell me if you can —

How does ocean learn shore

Is there something infinitely

Knowable between the storm

And rainbow that must remain?

EVANGEL

When they sat in hushed silence
Before your precise incise words
Honed to a catching edge and
Spoken with crystal clarity they
Remained silent and seemed
Quite impressed even awed
Convinced that you were right.
You took many careful pains
Few could have been as sharp
So persuasive, so patient, so
Complete and it was obvious
They had no questions left since
Not a hand was raised or an
Eyebrow when you asked your
Several questions. Do you suppose,
Then, they were redeemed?
Once I heard a man say:
We have not converted a person just because we've shut her up.

THE BOMB

It blew and

Miles away there was no sound

Not for a while

It blew, gorgeously artistic

From a safe distance

It blew, tumbling things over and

Over from far away end over end

In anticipation of it arrival the

Earth stiffened, then yielded

A child blinked, whimpered and

Jerked, turning to instant

Powder.

NIGHT SO SOON?

He hoped and hoped

The *dawn* would rise and break

Upon his dreams and bring them

Early to pass. He watched for

Signs at *midday* to reap the

Harvest from long and intentional

Toil. He vowed he could delay his

Playtime. In the *afternoon* he would

Run and jump and laugh and play

Until *dark* came, or at least 'til

Sun's set filled to the brim with

Early evening leisure among his family.

What he had not planned on at all

Was on night coming so soon.

PLAYING IT COOL

His soul has been

Earthbound a while the

Friend of dormant flowers

Dried leaves and wintered

Trees. Not down and out

Neither bone dry in a way

But going on in routine

Days. He wonders, sort of

Where the feeling went that

Used to be. Neither bliss nor

Grief occupies the soul, but

Then, neither do pain and

Anguish... only a slight un-

Easiness at the prospect of

Being cool – not

Cold – as the way of life

He habitually chooses

TO JOHN AND MARTIN ET. AL.

Tell me if you can what
We'll do when all of them
Are gone
When they've been taken
One-by-one from us
Oh! They *are* gone
They've been gone
Taken one-by-one
But
When we knew them it was
Good!
Their vision and wisdom and
Courage
Painted dreams to
Create out of trumpeting
Chaos
But now we've learned the lesson
And it's hard – we need
Vision again, wisdom and courage
Again and it's not as much
Fun around here any more
As it used to be and it
Worries me
The lyrics and poems and cheers the
Smiles and songs and heroes they
Are legends now, or have simply
Gone to
Somewhere I'd rather be
John and Martin and Rosa and Dorothy et. al.

(cont'd)

They are the old and wise and our
Despair smells of human thugs and
Feral morphs dumping every good
So tell me if you can
What the lesson was we learned

I AM

I am what and who
I always was and
I will ever be
Since I was and
Am in the mind of
God
Nothing has changed
Before any thing
Or the foundation was
Or will change in the
Essence of me
I am the same
The no-different breath
Breathing in and breathing
Out of God
I am in the ideas of God from
Before suns shone
Or stars twinkled somewhere beyond
The start of today and ever will be
It is further than bliss to know
I was we are in the creative heart
In the thought of God way before the start
It could have been just now

AN ULTRA-THIN FILM

It is not fickle or fanciful
Though some may disagree
To draw an imaginary parallel
Between heaven and a moment's
Trout fishing on Montana's Smith River
Or many cold-water streams in the west
Or eastern states including Cripple Creek in Virginia
I noticed this from a print of forty years ago in
Hippers standing alongside a stream in up-
State New York – I and my spouse could
Hardly see me – I'd nearly disappeared
From her sight and mine though
She had snapped the photo
Across a distance of less
Than twenty feet
We, both of us
Could see it –
A film
We
Could see
Clear through it
To the 'other side'
Which were the same
Almost

IRAQ

I cannot remember its beginning
It isn't easy to see number one from
Number 9,855 and counting even if I try
Twenty-seven from eighty-three leave a trail
Of fifty-six when we lived and toiled in Colorado
On our way to Huber Heights and Avon, Indiana and
Then Gardiner beside the Yellowstone stopping then in TN
It cannot be but is years passing a
Long war or preparation for war or its
Cessation there is no stopping or resting
From more planning for and preparation of
Forever killing and murder and waste and devastation
No one can estimate not even the children and civilian toll of
The dying and mutilated and endless butchery and savage loss
Of humanity via
Poisoning
Multiple maladies
Death by sanctions
Bombs and myriad bullets
Missiles launched
Triggers pulled
Body bags filled
Bodies stilled
Forever
When was it we spoke of war
This is the war like there never
Was another war to end all wars

DOUBLE RAINBOW

Red
Orange
Yellow
Green
Blue
Indigo
Violet
Dark space
Violet
Indigo
Blue
Green
Yellow
Orange
Red
Over the Yellowstone
Above Dome Mountain
We stand hand-in-hand
Shaped by awe

YOU PAY

You pay for your poverty these days

If you're white and moderately affluent

And ready for action

$80 for jeans with authentic patches

Off the rack at Slick's Boutique

Strange empathy

Tie-dyed and sandled caring

Compassion a-go-go

KNOWING THE MYSTERY

I do not know how to tell you
Or how to say it
Words in any tongue could not express it
It being the inexpressible
Neither can it be described
It is, however, irrepressible
Like ones girl-child . . . or a rainbow
I can only try to speak it
And hope the beating of unseen wings
Can, also, be heard by you
If only faintly
I can stutter it sometimes or, perhaps, whisper it
Its soaring mystery does not depend on me
To get through
Maybe the light and love are enough
Maybe the Coming will say more
Than you or I could ever tell, or imagine
Were we to anticipate the highest, the deepest
And the best

SUCH SMALL GIFTS

Two smooth, white rocks
An oil canvas that I painted one time
As a young adult
The harmonica left by my favorite uncle
He died in 1974
The robin's nest that fell from a tree last summer
All my best marbles, with no chips
The deep blue and bright red ones are beautiful
Some special money: my three coins from Egypt
The soap sculpture of an elephant carved
By our daughter
The best pocketknife in the world . . .
One blade's broken
Our family's picture album with pressed flowers
Mostly dogwood inside
The Mickey Mouse wristwatch that stopped
Thirty-five years ago, or more
A very long chain of silver and gold paper clips
My report card from the year I made all-A's-but-one
The baseball glove that Dad used – I used it, as well
Our first son's first lock of fine, golden hair
A newspaper article with my name at the top
The children's toy drum
A jar of homemade apple jelly
Carol made it
These we bring, they are yours
Dearest Holy One

GOD'S BUSINESS

God's business is Reds
Oranges and Yellows
God's business is Greens
Blues, Indigos and Violets
I think God loves greens and blues best
God's business is beauty
Monarchs and God's other winged flowers
God's business is Singing in the night
Dancing in the light
Loving folk to life

GOD SPOKE JOHN 1:1-5

It was night - or, the next early morning, perhaps
Accompanied by a quelled, breathless sky
As ten-hundred billion wings, also, could not move, daring
Not a single flutter
The angels waited... 'til
I'M spoke: "Psst"
While myriads spirits leaned in to hear
The galaxies careened their ears
Toward the fathomless as a trillion
Suns blinked, their silence
Echoing beyond all worlds:
God's word is flesh
The stars, mute, quieter than mute turned
As if trying to listen, or
Thirsting to feel and taste and drink
And breathe in
The nature of being
Space itself bowed, eons
Clapped a standing ovation and, without ceasing
Creation, herself, could not anthem enough for
The smallest God-glory
Of all who
Opened two eyes, one at a time and
wiggled and sneezed in a hay trough.

AND WHEN HE COMES

And when he comes we will know or
Get to know, if we don't recall
Love has come
In late evening when
Stars are a-glitter twirling
And the world turns to face
Enormous light burning, burning
He comes early, in the dawn when
Hearts are young
And pounding
While men our hate employ
He comes in gently and speeds
Not away, but soul-ward
And when we meet we will
Know we've met somewhere before and
We'll surely be gathered to
Fly merrily around the moon to
Forever.

THE FLY OF WINTER'S END

I saw a fly of winter's end
Its wings were dragging slowly
Down the faded curtain's bend
It seemed a thing quite holy

To see a simple creature go
Without one jumpy nerve
But smoothly, patiently descend
The winter curtain's curve

It puzzled me, a six-year old
How such creatures do survive
A thought arose and it was bold
That God wants flies to thrive

I asked God with no shame
Or pause of voice at all
If God gives flies a special name
Because they're short, not tall

"No," replied the God who loves
"I want the earth to see
God, also, loves the winter doves
And all the creatures that be."

Then I, with quiet and stilled breath
Sat wondering and moved
For God, with subtle, gentle stealth
Has convinced me: I am loved.

Prayers

$\mathcal{T}$he prayers included in this book are the writer's personal feelings and responses stimulated by the biblical Book of Psalms, as they were translated and interpreted in Eugene Peterson's *The Message*. *The Message* is a complete Bible which was translated into English by the late teacher-scholar and pastor, Peterson. *The Message* is not a word-for-word translation of the original languages of the Ancient and New Testaments – Hebrew, Greek and Aramaic – but translates the original texts into contemporary English and is meant to convey the modern American's way of speaking, hearing and understanding the English language. I regard Peterson's translation as 'translating for meaning.' The so-called exact translations of the sacred text result in stilted and often awkward constructions, in lost meaning and difficult word flow. The present writer's preference has been to grasp as much of the intent of the Psalter as is personally possible and to respond, argue, retort, react and communicate his own personal sense of reality, his experience and feelings in relation to human life in the early twenty-first century.

Taken as a whole, the prayers written number 550, or so. Their intent is to be conversational – the prayers herein included are some of the author's most personal and deeply considered of the entire collection. Will you, the reader, pray them as they are written, with openness and expectancy. Perhaps you will, also, choose to read the Psalm to which the prayer is replying. This will help you lean into both Psalm and prayer in, perhaps, positive ways and to get glimpses into the heart of the psalmist.

How is any child of God, as I am, to enter conversation and relationship with Creator God? After his first fifty years of living, it became clear to this responder that I had always been in conversation and personal relationship with the One Who Is.

The prayers of this work are, I think, representative of the entire collection. My experience in praying is a daily and on-going reality, although I am not conscious of its being "prayer" most, or even much of the time. It's a labor, a practice, a being, a life in thanksgiving, a trek of attempting openness and experiencing frequent puzzlement ... as well as, at times, more than a little *angst*. This sacred passage through the life of prayer is a long pilgrimage "in the same direction" (a paraphrase of one of Dr. Peterson's book titles).

-Lee Anglin

PSALM ONE
"Still struggling, Lord"

God, I'm struggling. I keep having the urge to gripe: How can some people *think* the way they think? The jazz lyrics have it: "Man, how can you *think* that way?"

But Lord, mine is reversed *bigotry*. Arrogant people deeply annoy me. And all I'm *left* with is, it is what it is! How can I sort *that* out? I'd *ask* you to *forgive* ... but I've come no where *near* honest repentance; I certainly *haven't* changed my mind and don't know if I will. I don't believe I *can* change this shady side of me, even with a lot of help. I just can't make myself *agree*. It feels like too much compromise? *I don't like snobs*, or bullies, or stuffed shirts, or braggarts, or the pompous and especially the self-important.

Jesus, *you* know my spirit. You know *I'm* warped, too; I *confess* I'm biased and narrow-minded. I see and live through scratched lenses, myopic eyes, spiritual narrowness. *I*, also, have walked in the dark midnights of ethical failure while *pretending* to be a high-road pilgrim. I've lived a nice *surface* life while all the while covertly stumbling along a low-road life of condemning, sentencing and executing others with my closed mind and sunless heart. It's called *hypocrisy*, dear Christ. I know.

Help! I *want* to hunger for your strong mind and loving power and for the lift of saints – will I ever move, Lord, in the direction of your humble, transforming love?

PSALM ONE
"Teach me…"

I'm learning, Father, that spending our *days* loving you and living for you *is* life. Living our lives knowing your love is *forever* life. Once I didn't know I was made for you. Now I'm desperate for you. I can't live a minute without you; I cannot take a breath without your love and grace.

For this, God, I am grateful. *Create* in me a perennially thankful heart.

Many are the ways you come to us; by *each* of them you have opened your Grace-Kit, pulled your healing out, applied the restoring love-balm and *awakened* our clouded eyes to you. Open us all to your Jesus-*way*. Give us enough of his resurrecting love to start your *new*-life in these our wounded, vacant hearts. You can do it, Lord. We trust you. Thank you for knowing how to find us, no matter where we were and are.

PSALM ONE
"As a last resort…"

Perhaps you've looked deeply and thought long about it, Teacher, but it doesn't appear to bother you any that many of us have come to you only as a last resort. What seems to matter to *you* is that we've come. We're *sure* that's the case, and that heaven right **now** is a happy, jumping place! But, let us say it straight, Lord: we are forever grateful the great thanksgiving is not *for us*! It's really for YOU, Lord, and your grace! How wonderful is *that*!

Thank you for not keeping time clocks on us and for not being irritated by our slowness. We know, Lord: our lives would have been supremely better had we said, "Yes!" to you early and often.

Let me say it: *here* is how we want to be like you: sparing no cost for the sake of another; sparing no effort or time spent in your service. Being kind and patient among our friends. All of it because of you: You *are* love.

PSALM TWO
"Why the big noise, nations?"

God, you're a saint! Why *aren't* you constantly piqued with us and our nation? How *sad* our attempts to deceive you, ourselves and *others* ... how *futile* our pompous pride. We're blinded, Lord, imagining our brand of "Christian" is better than any Muslim, or atheist, or just about everybody else! Our nation's ego is near an impenetrable *darkness*, the *antithesis* of how we prefer to think of ourselves: inviting and generous to a fault. We announce, "America is the most generous country in the world!" While our transcontinental *arrogance* is, in truth, a blasphemous slap in God's and every body else's face.

Occasionally, *we* see it, too: sometimes as a *nation* we *know* we stink. Is it possible we *don't* anger you, Lord? "We're *more* special!" "*We're* Number One!" "U.S.A.! U.S.A.!" "Mirror, mirror on the wall...?" What's **this** about, Lord? Why do we keep pushing for rank, snatch at prominence and scuffle for position? Why do we *posture* so, *ignoring* the restraining *boundaries* that true living for you implies?

The psalmist says, God *"breaks out laughing"* at our conceit and bullying. It makes good sense that you *laugh*, Father - rather than cry. But you do *weep*, don't you, Yahweh? Our grandiosity breaks your *heart*, doesn't it? *Yours* is the wounded smile of grace-filled love.

Our cry, Lord, our souls thirst for the gentle power of your love to change and forgive us. Make us, we pray, a *repentant* nation, people and persons. Do your kind work in us to make us humble, generous and kind. Change our national mind one-hundred eighty degrees to peace making. Empower us to live *forgiven* and *forgiving* lives. Inside us there's hunger for true godliness.

PSALM TWO
"Fear and trembling"

Lord, "in trembling awe" I'm celebrating Messiah. You declare (and I paraphrase), "I know you'd prefer to kiss your *own* rings. But, hear me," says YHVH, "your need is to 'kiss the signet of God's Messiah'." It is to bow at the feet of the Holy Christ of God, to offer brilliant praise to God-Immanuel, to lay your hearts and minds down before God-man. O Christ of God, I do this with gladness and thanks-giving. Forgive, Lord, my reticence; heal my awkward resistance.

By your great grace, flowing like a *river*, God, grant today that *we* may make a run for you with stamina, dive deeply into your Way and begin our swim in your vast ocean, eternal life. So be it in me and us now and forever. Yes.

PSALM TWO
"Demagogues and delegates…"

Dear God! I'm glad and thankful you created us. I don't know why, or how, or when, or where you did it – but I'm *glad* you did it. I don't know how such *variety* in the human family happened, but I'm thrilled it did and still does. Thank you for the myriad differences you've fashioned and breathed into these lives of flesh and spirit.

It's not easy for me to own the truth, Lord, that we, your *children*, make utter messes of things, some of them massive. We've trashed much of your creation. We keep building bigger dumps every place we land, including outer space and the oceans. But, we're *your* creatures and not one of *us* is trash, even if we act like we are. Thank you that not one of us will *be* trashed. Not by you. You *made* us by your love and I don't believe you're even a little bit sorry about that. We make messes of your banquet hall and engage our food fights at table. We wear ourselves out in aggressiveness and waste ourselves in utter foolishness. J. Weldon Johnson said, 'We *slip* and *slide*, and *slip* and *slide* until we bang our heads up against hell's iron gate' (paraphrased).

I confess it, Lord! We incline toward the ludicrous. We work our schemes. We spin our webs. We lie through our teeth. We thump our chests and celebrate empty bravado! How *silly* is that, Lord! We can be a rough crowd, it seems to me, but we can't "box with God." Our minds and arms are too short.

Yet, Lord… I know something *else*: you're not far from us. Many here have heard the whisper of your eternity and answered, "Thank you! Use me, Lord!" Again and again and again some have come near and said, "Yes, Lord!" It keeps *happening* and heaven keeps rocking!

So, rather than endlessly *fret* over the messes we make, Lord, give us *your* undaunted courage, that we may love you and *delight* in your Kingdom with our brothers and sisters. Re-freshen the *rejoicing* spirits in us that we may assist, serve, lift and bless all you have made. Keep re-storing in us the *gladness* to bear you *happy* witness and joyful self-giving in your name among earth's peoples.

PSALM THREE
"Enemies sprouting like mushrooms?"

Why do I have so few *enemies*, Lord? Right now I can't think of *one*. There surely *are* some who don't *like* me, who want nothing to do with me. But, *enemies*? For instance, I can't name one who despises me because of the love or magnetism of my faith. I *suspect* I know why.

I've made a *career* of not *making* enemies. I prefer to be liked; love to be appreciated. There *are* a couple hands-full who dislike my politics, a few who don't care for my social inclinations. But, spiritual *'enemies sprouting like mushrooms'* because of my powerful heart for *God?* I know not one.

I'd probably *provoke* some people, were I openly vocal about following Jesus. It's a lock people would back off if Bible verses were continually spouting from my lips. But, I wouldn't *do* that. It's not in me to *look* for ways to make enemies on behalf of my faith.

Father, the *real* reason I have few-to-no enemies is *this*: I'm unlike *you*; I'm near the image of most of the people around me. I blend in. I'm one of them. I'm unlike Jesus. If I were more like *him*, it would be much different, I'm almost sure. Jesus *said* people who love him *will* be *opposed* and persecuted, that loving *his ways* and doing them will *equal* conflict.

God, I admit that *some* folk irk *me* more than a little – namely the ones who *think* they look, act and are very much like you. (God, let *me* somehow live into the certainty that *no* one irks you.)

This is the person I want to become: one who is respected and appreciated by persons who need you most ... a person who *lives* the truth that my present and eternal needs can be met only by you ... a man who unpretentiously and unconsciously reminds others *of* you, at least once in a while ... someone who practices daily *being* like you. Indeed.

PSALM THREE
"Hearing"

It seems I sometimes have to *shout* to get your attention, Lord. A *friend* said God **may** indeed have an auditory *blockage* where he (my friend) is concerned. He added: he'd never *once* felt a nudge or hint of God's *real* presence.

There have been times *I've* wondered if you *are* – it's an awkward thing to admit. Just today someone said to me, "I don't think God gets involved in the every-day lives of people; things just happen. God may exist, but isn't really here for us." Could it be, Lord? Could that be the case?

But ... I will still call to you, Jesus, and thank you. *Not* "just in case" you're real. No. I *have* decided. I will trust you and wait for you, even when my spirit falters and my faith wanders. Yes! God is with me! God is *with* us. I've come to believe God is *most* intensely with us when we have no sense of God being with us, at all.

PSALM THREE
"A second listen"

I heard an older holy woman say, "It gets lonely in this skin. **But**," she added, "*I've* mulled it and pondered it and concluded: it's really not *God* who's absent, or deaf. *God* has neither a hearing nor an answering problem. *We're* the ones with lazy ears and vacationing minds." That seems, Lord, a more viable truth. The impediments to reception are *we*. With such clash and clamor inside, it's not easy to hear God's silence, or even to start listening.

Lord, I've wondered: living with the likes of *us*, haven't you found yourself at times totally speechless? Aren't there times and occasions when there's nothing even *you* can say?

Is the truth plainly this: *we* don't *want* to *hear* God speak to us of a deep *life commitment*, of sacrificial love, or serious discipleship? Just don't want to *hear* God speak of unflinching obedience. Blessing, yes! Change, **no**! We don't *want* to change, not much, at least not enough to make a real difference in how we live our lives.

The real question, God, is not "Do you hear *us*?" or "Do you care?" It is, "Do *we* hear you? Do we *want* to hear? Are we *listening*?"

Lord, what's the *meaning* of the *silence* I hear? Have I required you to speak to me in clear American? Do I need to learn to listen ... to speak less and be still more, to rest before you and not try to think of things to say in response ... to be genuinely patient? Are there words to hear within your silence?

PSALM THREE
"His answers thunder?"

Are there wrong and right *ways* to pray? It seems to me now that living, itself, is praying.

I seldom ask you for personal favors, Lord. I mostly thank God for the joy of living and the hope of doing it faithfully. I'm most comfortable praying for others. Is this a short sighted way to practice the discipline of conversation with you, quiet Spirit? Is my relationship with you neither tall nor deep enough for me to feel free to ask? *Should* I seek *more* personal blessing although I'm mostly satisfied with you all the time? The biblical book of *James* says we don't receive because we don't *ask*. I figure this probably means we are to be asking mostly on behalf of others.

The *psalmist* shouts, "His answers *thunder*!" Which sounds like God's responses are spiritual fireworks, *right there* for *any* one to hear!

I'm *thanking* you, God! When praying with words, I usually don't hear words; however, I thrill with the conviction that you *answer*. You listen and *hear* and care, *not* from *high heaven*; *you're* nearer than the air we breathe. Closer than the cells in our bodies. No, I *don't* receive out-loud, clear-channel messages. There's no private, secure line between just the two of us; although, I *really* believe there *is* such a gift for everyone.

When I'm praying, Father, my arm hair hardly ever stands on end. But, Lord, there IS *thunder* … I've heard God *thunder twice*, when God said, *"I have claimed you for my own."*

Finally, for the ones who think they've never heard your voice, but love and serve you, any way, *that's* some kind of beautiful thunder. Amen

PSALM FOUR
"God is our more-than-enough."
(A public prayer)

You are our Provider, Life's *Breath* Giver. Giver of rivers of grace. Giver of mercies unnumbered.

Grace us now. Mercy us, we ask. Keep the showers of your transforming presence pouring on us, that we may see and hear you more clearly and follow you more graciously. *Covenant* us *again*, for we keep forgetting.

It's late now, but we see how we've strayed from the path you walked. Born for holiness we, instead, have been silly. We've *lived* as sinners and continued to misshape your life in us by mental laziness, spiritual apathy and personal fears ... hearts of darkness are still our frequent habitat.

Holy God, we keep imagining that having more *stuff* marks real accomplishment and the guarantee of happiness. We *don't* broadcast it, but we live it. Will a person be blessed when she has *all she ever wanted?* Will we ever be satisfied with having what we *need?* Will endless grasping make us *gentler* souls? Teach us, Lord, that a daily grind of climbing and scuffling for more are not *good* things.

You have shown us greatness: your thrilling creation, your reconciling kindness, your servant humility. Greatness in us is the living *relationships* you provide and we enjoy; it's the out-pouring of your quiet providing. Your revealing presence keeps us near heaven and draws us together, showing us the way of eternal life.

Teach us *how* to live thankfully until we *do*, how to live joyfully with all you provide. Grateful, we are learning that *true greatness*, though un-common in occurrence, is *God* bringing and keeping life and hope and people together in mutual servanthood. Why, Lord, would we prefer more stuff to this? Yes, Sir!

PSALM FIVE
"I lay out the pieces..."
(Read first paragraph very slowly)

I bow naked before you, Lord – covering, as is my habit, a few ugly spots. Here *are* the pieces of my life – the hours and moments, this temporary body called 'home,' the work I do, the deep and the shallow relationships, my thoughts and thankfulness, the talents you keep giving and I keep not using well, the attitudes both hopeful and sinful in me ... *all* the conglomerate, the fragments and cells, the *sum* of *me*. Here they are, hoping to be cleansed, needing to be purified, wanting to be perfected as day succeeds day.

I've done *enough* mischief, truth bending and sin wallowing to go around, God. I've asked: "How *is* it you reject *it* but not me? How do you sponge the whole into your love? How is it possible you continue to grace me and us?" I'll never understand, although I will keep trying and continue to *ask* for it and appreciate it. I want always to be thankful. I've come to imagine you don't reject the mistakes, the broken promises, my shoddy attitudes or secret miscues. Your compassion, I'm starting to believe, can transform anything.

There's too much good in you to measure, Lord: the ability you give us to be sensitive and sad and embarrassed; the longing you implant in us for you that will not die; the joy of lasting friendships between male and female, male and male in which *you're* the source and adhesive. For great books, the sun's brilliance and life-empowering things to do. Lord, thank you!

But what's *most* wonderful about you, Jesus, is: you receive, accept, chow down and socialize with the wicked; theologians and preachers call it God's "condescension," God bending low. I doubt you consider it that. The instant we invite you to our party, you're already dancing. You keep hunting ways to enter our shuttered hearts; you'll come in by a side door, or the bathroom window, if that's what we leave ajar. Your truth *destroys* our lies without destroying *us*. On a hill far away and nearer than our skin, hanging between two guys like me, you *come* squarely into our sin-wallow and soak up all the mud and dirt and grime in your cleansing embrace. How beautiful!

You're breathtaking! You make life eternal and reshape the cries of our hearts into ballads of joy.

For that, Lord, our thankful *words*, while good, cannot suffice. A lifetime – and then some – of living for *you* is our call. Thus, such as we are, we gladly offer ourselves to you now. And we stand, amazed! Heaven and earth are a banquet of celebration to you!

PSALM SEVEN
"...furious enemies"

It's bone-wearying, Lord! The human family bumps, pounds and stomps one another. So much cutting and slashing! Friend betrays friend; enemies kill enemies. Humanity growls, "Never mind God! We'll do it *our* way, live *our* truth, choose *our* life; you, there, God, *don't* interfere! Don't mess with us. We're just fine."

Don't you think it's decidedly time, Lord, to get hold of things? Take the mess in *your* own hands? Stand up and *put* up for once, instead of *shutting* up in silence. *Show* up, Lord! *Give* the world your what-for! In *certain* terms show us again exactly *who*'s boss. Say it: "I AM *GOD!* AND I MEAN IT!" Write it across the sky! For once, could you be just a little more sharp-edged, hard-nosed and *obvious*?

The psalmist says, "*Nobody* gets away with *anything*" (my emphasis). Was he joking? He must be thinking, "in the *long* run." *That's*, perhaps, how it is. It's a different *crisis* every day in these United States. And, I'm telling you, if one doesn't intervene, we'll *create* a couple, ourselves!

I doubt a graphic video of homo sapien life today *would* look like Camelot. Why don't you just rear up and put a stop to the nonsense? Do it and your reputation will skyrocket! Give it some thought. Once in a while, Lord, don't you have the urge to use a tad more muscle?

Another thought keeps niggling at me, Lord. Is it *possible* – being in *this* world right now, where living is so much rip-and-tear, where men are left for dead, where only a relative few bother to care – is it *possible* you're "toughening us up and gentling us down for servant-hood, probing our weakness with your love, knocking off our roughest edges, making us the *compassionates*" ... so that, no matter what comes, whatever happens, no matter the contingencies, we become fit and able and *truly* human? If this *be* the case, Lord, Amen!

PSALM SEVEN
"Mischief backfires, violence boomerangs"

As I've said often, Lord, *sin-life* confounds me. There's no denying I'm a sinner, part of the whole. What baffles me is: are there *grades* of sin with you? Large numbers of religious people say there are. But, in your mind, can sin be graded and *classified*? In the Gospels, Jesus doesn't indicate this or that sin is greater, or more damaging than another. But is murder not worse than shoplifting? Is incest equal in gravity to roadway speeding? If it is, the reasons are shrouded in my brain. If I say to someone, "I'll pray for you," but don't follow through on my promise, will that be *as* sinful in *God's* eyes as becoming angry with someone and injuring him verbally or physically?

God, if I *act* in such ways that another person is helped and encouraged, would it matter to *you* if I made a big show and dramatic scenario of it? If I served in order to *be admired*?

Without exception, is *every* human abortion the *same* to you? Does abortion *always* earn your negative judgment? There are religious souls who get their hackles up: "You're damned right, it does!" I say, "No, it doesn't." So, I'm really *interested* in how *Jesus* would answer.

How *is* it, Jesus, with the same breath a person will condemn all abortions, then agree that the death of a two-year old from a stray bomb or bullet is but an unhappy consequence of war, or the neighborhood, a necessary by-product of conflict ... particularly *if* the conflict be perpetrated by *our* side. Is that a ticket *you'd* punch, Lord? I say there's something creepy there. Something doesn't calculate.

Will a person fare better with *you*, Lord, if he kills someone called "the enemy" during war than if he kills his mate in a drunken, jealous rage?

Is *obesity* a sin, or a glandular deficiency? Is it but a human weakness you overlook? Do you have compassion toward persons with habitual over-eating problems?

Is legal divorce moral depravity? Is God, or can God be glorified when a marriage fizzles, but the couple keeps hanging on ... and on? If there's nothing left but estrangement, or a sterile existence between two human beings living *separately* in the same *'empty'* house, is that more pleasing to you than divorcing? Lord? Do you honor it when a man and woman stay in the same house until one of them dies, although they've despised each other the last thirty-five years? Is that *marriage*? In your eyes, if the *commitment* has died, are the two married, or divorced? Will there be stars in their crowns *because* they doggedly dug in and physically endured, although they slowly died inside?

I wish I knew, Lord. I don't think I'm asking 60 silly questions, like, "How many angels can stand on the head of a pin?"

Can *actual* adultery sometimes occur when there is no *physical* infidelity? Is adultery exclusively the act of sleeping with someone other than ones spouse? Or is despising ones spouse, also, adultery? Is there more to it than an illicit sex act?

We humans, Lord, are tempted to over-simplification, living with judgmental spirits, and confusing *our* moral positions with the more *important* issues of human existence. So, teach us this: we *are* limited sinners, all of us and God's passionate love for us is the power that sets us free. Lord, don't give up on us.

PSALM EIGHT
"… brilliant, brilliant Lord"
(A public prayer)

God, the rocks *do* cry, "Hosanna!" *All* creation is blessed in your grace! The hills shake, roll and reverberate with your joyful music! You are Spirit-*ever*-near; to you our humble delight and gratitude are lifted in song and silence!

You are Creator of universe, galaxies, our earth-home, Afghanistan, Nashville, Gardiner MT … we shower hallelujahs heavenward; we offer unceasing thanksgiving to high heaven!

You are God of fierce grizzly, helpless lamb and noisy grasshopper … to *you* universal awe is owed! You make good things that work for life's good. This gathered community bows before you now and rejoices in God our Savior! Your *human* children may at times not be much to look at – but, then, I will mention Sir Peacock, Master Gazelle – but you've purposed *us* to be your stewards of the earth. Ah! Lord, your love for us is lovely.

You have made vast and deep oceans and quiet streams … Sequoia and Forget-me-not … you are wonderful God of bright discoveries and dark nights of the soul … You are Poet of life's *dance*, Giver of eternal blessing, Master of the grand mystery of God-love … how *glad* is our song, "You the Lord *are* our God!"

PSALM NINE
"Telling God stories"

What are the stories of God we need to tell this generation, Lord? Do you want the ones voicing God's anthems to highest mountain, or those quietly sung that even children may hear and meet God without fright or fear? Will we sing and speak to encourage new players: "come, get in God-shape," or to warn, self-importantly, "you don't deserve to play in *our* game?" Shall we, in every circumstance, live the God-life with thanksgiving, or shout warnings and predictions about the world's "one-way ticket to hell?" Will we spend our brief days stabbing our fingers, trashing others' reputations and continuously shouting the coming perdition of the godless?

No! Lord! No! *We're* thanking God from full hearts and we will not relent. We're whistling God tunes, and offering God-stories for *Christ* joy! We're telling God's book of wonders in ways the world can hear and understand! We will be God's safe-house saga for the beaten, the burned out and battered.

Lord, make *us*, if you will, your human word to the worn out and beaten up; construct with *us* your ode of blessing for lonely folk and the spiritually homeless. Create in us believable stories of tender mercies for the up-tight and stressed out. We'd like to be your living volume of balm and calm for those stretched beyond limits. Make us true God-passages for any who continually get the short end of society's stick. In short, Lord, pour your compassion in us and let volumes of love spill out to bathe the world-worn and walking-dead.

Build among us a *global* library where no humiliation occurs, where no one is left to fend by himself and where every person's story is included. Work your creative love through us, please – so that there be no one left outside.

We're "singing your song, High God!" You are the poet and author!

PSALM ELEVEN
"Going to hell in a hand basket"

Do some in every generation live by the same prognosis: "The world's going to hell in a hand basket"?

Lord, what shall *we* say, we who attempt to live by faith? The saccharin optimist says, "This is the best of all possible worlds!" The dour pessimist, wryly smirking, responds, "I'm afraid you're right!"

I refuse, Father, to live either up Baby Blossoms Lane or down Paranoid Gulch. I have faced opposition and it was more than uncomfortable. I've been made a laughing-stock, the object of lies, slander and gossip. A few *brothers* and *sisters* were once determined to shame and ostracize me. They thought they were on to something juicy. What they *said* happened was hearsay taken to the third power.

I will not claim innocence or guiltlessness of wrongdoing, God. Neither will I run or hide from your great adventure. Opposition will not cower or sour me … the life you are and have given is much too beautiful and intoxicating for that.

Why, God, will I not give in or give up? Because – even if the sky falls or the bottom collapses, and should it appear your followers don't have a chance, *you* haven't run or moved "to the mountains" or suburbs. *You are not* enjoying a long-needed vacation at your out-of-the-fray hideaway.

You're still *here*; you have this child's and all your children's backs. So, *right here* is where I want to be. I'll pitch my tent in your camp … at least some of the time.

PSALM ELEVEN
"...straight in the eye"

I'm not so sure I want or need to look you straight in the eye, Father. As you know, I'm not bold, any more, or a risk-taking person. My beloved mentor, Marney, *spoke* boldness into me forty-five years ago and it 'took'. Since moving to retirement *eighteen* years ago, however, the old introverted me has resurfaced and I've become more reticent to act boldly or take risks. I haven't sorted it, but I think the *large* part of me now is, perhaps, overly concerned with not wanting to appear judgmental, or harsh towards other souls. I'm more apt now to be quiet and prefer listening to talking – boldly, or otherwise.

Lord, I'm not declaring myself now a thoughtful contemplative and, by no means a bona fide mystic. I pray more personally than ever, but with many fewer words. Lately I've found it good simply to point my 'pointy' finger 'heavenward' and speak the name of the person who is in some way needing your special attention – for example pointing and saying, "Diane" – or pointing and saying "Please bless Nathan and use me to help if you must – I am willing." Most of the time presently I don't even point.

To be honest, I think this sort of 'shorthand' praying fits my temperament, more than many words do.

When you became a man, Lord, the essence of it was (and *is*) that you knelt, bowed, bent low – not to demean yourself, but to show us you are friendly. You were born baby Jesus, and who would not love a baby? When you could see, you looked Mother Mary in the eye and your *eyes* said, "Here I am for you to nurture, to bless and to be blessed, as well as to enjoy."

God, after all these years of wanting to love and bless you with my mind and my life, it's still a stretch to be comfortable looking you 'straight in the eye". That's a bit much for me. I believe I could manage it with *Jesus*, although I'm aware he is you and you are he. I wouldn't be *fearful*, not with you, Father God, but somehow "Father" feels bigger and a little more distant. When I think, "Father God," I kind of want to *bend parts* of me low in your direction. "Standing tall" in your presence seems a stretch.

PSALM TWELVE
"The last decent person just went down…"

To me, Lord, this psalm is a pure genius analysis of our times. There *are precious few* in the milling crowd to command high trust. Where *are* the heroes of righteousness, the heroines of kind-living? Where can authentic truth-champions be found? Each of us knows a few – maybe a *handful.* But I *despair* the paucity of *living models* for both young and old populating our land.

Celebrities are often little more than blowfish. Professional athletes are frequently pampered-brats and narcissists. Politicians talk in lie-language through "oily lips." Generals spout double-speak to advance the warring madness. The nation is replete with fork-tongued media moguls who obfuscate the facts and make an art of prevarication. Big-Four banks are greedy thieves; they are snatch-and-grab misers. Our national *leaders* do whatever it takes to feather their own nests, while they egregiously *skimp* on lifting a hand to help people from the bottom of the heap. *Wanting more* is the common language of Century 21. The powerful take from the weak and give it to the richest. Where *have* the good ones gone? Have the 'good ones' always been a relative few?

Lord, you *know* there aren't *any* who are good, *not* as God is good. There is *none* like *God*, not *one*: not King, or Einstein, or Truth, or Bonhoeffer; neither Teresa, nor Lincoln, nor even mom.

Multiple are the reasons to *echo* David's vision of a wicked world filled with scurvy people. The world *is* a place of surpassing evil; death and darkness appear to reign.

I, too, have *hidden* my glowing candle rather than let its joyful light burn for all to see. I, also, live under a bushel of trepidation and hesitation.

I am prone to grasp David's view: the world *is* a Legion of shabbiness, a place of exceeding stygian iniquity … but…

With David I, also, declare (in the *midst* of darkness): the *Lord* is pure love and there's not a shadow of darkness in him. Sometimes, loving

Creator, I scarcely can manage being positive for two hours in a row. It is *difficult* to see or believe God is going to win.

PSALM THIRTEEN
"I've looked at the back of your head long enough."

I've already blamed you for more things than I can count, Lord. Most of all I have complained that you neither hear, see, nor care. But I have decided: *never again.*

The troubles I've seen, what seems a large bag of grief, the pain — mostly now seem *self*-inflicted. Pretending you have no heart for *me* – *that*, Father, is over and done.

It's gone. It's *not* the back of your head I've grumbled of not seeing; it's *my* refusal to recognize you presence straight-on and looking at me. I *don't* trust you deeply; it's sad, I know.

I have determined to look *to* you with *new* eyes; already my heart has begun to sing. I *think* the song and singer are you.

I am asking, Jesus: transplant something that lives in you into me. I want to see as you see. I want your eternal *kind* of love to live in me. New eyes, new mind, new heart, *your* heart living in me. Amen

PSALM FOURTEEN
"Treating people like a fast-food meal…"

Sadly, Lord, many of us, your people live as if there is no hope. Thus some of us treat *others* like they're nobodies. We act like even our *brothers* and *sisters* are hardly more than "fast-food" meals to be taken in and quickly digested, as we hasten on to more palatable fare.

But *you*, Lord Christ, treat *us* as royalty. You see us whole and *real* and act as if we are your delight. Your love for us is miraculous, greater far than when you changed the water to wine. You change *us* … from *self*-centered to *you*-centered, from *me centered* to others-centered, from warriors to peacemakers, from instruments of darkness into reflections of your great Light. One. Two. Three… THANKS!

Thank God in heaven: we are *not* our own, not *on* our own, not *for* our own selves alone. *You*, God, are for us; and we are learning we never need to live for ourselves. Make us the way you are.

Alone, on our own, Lord, warrior generations quickly become toothless and eyeless. But God, your business is the remaking industry: you recreate human snarls into songs, growls into carols of hope, our self-focused laments into saints singing good for the neighborhood.

By *your* transforming mercy, it's *not* an "eye-for-an-eye or tooth-for-tooth world". There *is* one who *saves* us from our old sad selves: You, saving God! Life-Changing God! You stand our lives right-side-up and turn our darkness to Light. *Love* is what you do. You, God, transfigure all humanity's death marches into pilgrimages of abundant living.

Praise God *always*! Praise *God always!*

PSALM FIFTEEN
"Blacklisted?"

Jesus, I never thought for a moment – not *ever* – that you blacklisted, excluded, or ignored any one … not after I became a follower and not, also, when I was a pagan. When I paid *no* attention to God, I nevertheless knew, or at least always sensed you were near everyone. Admittedly, I thought my thoughts were just the ignorant imaginings of someone from the 'sticks' who fantasized too much what was probably untrue. I didn't have a church (didn't really care for mom's church [it had no black children and my best friend was black]) and, besides, my life was swept up in athletics and sports – mostly baseball, football, basketball, tennis, fishing, hunting, scouting, rambling the woods, hunting arrowheads … and doing it *all* with dad. Here I am, Lord, informing you, as if you don't already know!

But I thought *some* about you and predominantly about the one mom called "Heavenly Father" and I could not imagine an abandoning, absentee, or indifferent such a one. I queried, but it did not compute.

Jesus, I've tried not to make too much of it. But I *have* wondered about my close connection and relationship with my dad and the almost lifelong conviction that you, Lord, have no human enemies; that even the ones to whom you are *their* enemy, are not *your* enemies. And Jesus, Master and Mentor, who *you* were took God to the cross and confirmed it – at least for me – that, if a person does *not* 'walk right, act right and live truth,' *you* will *never* kick him out, or ignore her, or exclude any from your great love.

For me that was a loud, "Wow!"

PSALM SIXTEEN
"My choice is you, God …"

Long before I knew you, millenia before I was, *your* heart beat for me. As it did for billions of God-creations. You imagined me, neither better nor worse than Adam, but unique, nevertheless. There is *one* of me and it was your imagination that brought me into being. There will never be another like me, or like any of the myriads you have created. See, Lord, I don't believe in reincarnation, although it's not such a bad idea.

Eons before I chose you, Eternal One, I was in your mind – before the galaxies were brought forth – deeply part of your bounding, pulsing compassion.

As a young man I said to you, "Lord and Master! Without you nothing makes sense."

My choice is you, God of Jesus, Jesus of God. Day and night my heart's urge is to stick with you. You are first and only in the universe. I have been being made by Great Joy. I am *your* choice, too. Jubilant inside-out-outside-in, thrilled through and through!

You have these feet on your *path* forever – I'm radiant from the shining of your shadow. Since you took my heart, I've been singing on the right road (by and large) and I've *wanted* to be a vital servant-child (a lot of the time).

Lord, don't let me, or anyone go. Don't let go, *especially* when we're weak, out of our depth, off the path, or just too mule-headed to *stay* on it. Never let go, *especially* when we're *strong*, at the top of our game, on top of the world. That's an "Amen".

PSALM SEVENTEEN
"… examine me from inside out…"

I've made a mark, Lord; people say I am a man of peace. They don't *know* me, do they, but I've no argument to raise. They're *partly* right. "Guilty, as charged!" The evidence does not lie, although it may be somewhat skewed. People see in me a peaceable man. That's both the image and life-truth I want to live.

But, Lord, as I yield myself to *you*, the One who has perfect vision, whose eyes' only lens is love and are faultless, I'm asking *you* to look me over and within, head to toe, core to peel.

I want living to be neither *my* way nor the *world's*. The hunger is: make the pilgrimage I'm on go *your* way, your world's way in me, Dear Master. I want to walk *your* genus and species walk, to stay on your path, to follow as faithfully as is within me to do. I yearn to be of *your* ilk.

Keep me on *your* well-marked trail. Let me trace your steps until I'd know them anywhere. Lord, you know *me* as you know the Father. Make your heartbeat mine. Show me your way until it's my habit. Live your true-love life in me by loving your *children* through me, just as *you've* loved them forever.

Paint your grace-graffiti on every path, trail and roadway of my life. Free *me* from fear, as I dwell in this world. Liberate me from any semblance of indifference, boredom or shallow worship and obedience.

Use me as you see fit until you're done with me. And, Lord, I'm thinking you would like to say right about now, "Lee, try to get over yourself some these next few years…"

PSALM SEVENTEEN
"The most honest prayer"

You've known this earth-child more than 30,000 days, Creator God. I wonder how many of them I have lived with pure integrity, or unblemished honesty. Perhaps the question is moot, and it doesn't matter in the life-long path of being. Still I *wonder*. Baby years don't count, I guess, but I've a four-year-old memory that hasn't abandoned me. As a *six*-year-old, I recall *wanting* to be honest with mom and dad; there were many 'slips' that were more than innocent fibs or flubs.

So, when I read David's words in their *Message* rendition, "the most honest prayer you'll ever hear..." first I did a slow smile and responsively shook my head; then I chuckled out loud. Impossible! I thought, *"What* a self-deceiver ... or *liar!"* Truth is, David did a pretty good job of deceiving his self, as well as of lying through his teeth more often than once. We two are more than *somewhat* alike.

But, I have chosen to give David 'space' here, Lord. Not because I'm nice, or generous, but because I'd want that from him. He says, "the most honest prayer *you'll ever hear."* Here's some slack. David, as I, liked to think of his self as an honest human being, maybe even as honest as we humanoids come. Maybe *this* is his point. Among family, friends, fellow warriors and others in high places, David may have *been* an exemplar of honesty... most of the time. Not pristine forever, not with no flaw. Making the honest *effort*.

I don't imagine I will ever *think I* occupy one of the high places among honest prayers in the human family, or have the purest and most genuine motives and thoughts, or be among the most honest with God, my brothers, sisters, or neighbors. At this moment my strong *intent* is to be honest, live honestly among men and women, pray without guile and relate openly and with integrity with God and the persons in my daily life. That has some validity in me now, I believe. Of course, not every time, or always.

PSALM EIGHTEEN
"I love you, God – you make me strong."

I've learned a thing or two, Lord. One is, it's *all* about *you*, not me. I need major help, Father, to get and keep the order *straight*. It's *about* God and God's never-ending love. It's about the Lord's mercy making new things happen for good. It's about the awe God generates in *us*, as in *all* who have hearing ears and hearts.

I'm profoundly *glad* that, while you *could* have, you didn't stay silent, God, but *spoke* your Word of life to make humankind and all creation new. Your Word *speaks* life eternally. I'm happy you did not leave us in the dark, or leave us alone to try to figure the important things out for ourselves. You spoke the clearest Word ever spoken – you still *do* – that souls like I may hear and worship and become and bless.

I've, also, learned to *be* silent and to wait… on your love, Lord. And to be thankful. I ask: for what is there not to be thankful? I'm *thankful*, Lord, and I'd welcome an extension to this grateful heart *long* enough to become a stronger, nobler steward in your Kingdom. Above all, I ask for your hand of teaching, that I may become genuinely, selflessly a loving man for God.

PSALM EIGHTEEN
"When I chased my enemies...."

Our ugly ideologies almost always seem to pop out of thin air (specifically, our heads), Lord. In majority, they usually seem trifling, petty, or mean and, I add, too numerous in political circles to number. The evidence is clear: our really hare-brained notions come from nowhere in particular and lead nowhere in general... except *downhill*, with no good purpose or intent. Am I missing something positive here, Lord? Often they are in truth groundless, paper-thin in substance, a universe separated from what is real; yet they cling like shoe dust to our minds and fly like spittle from our mouths. God, forgive.

It's a sad thing what we do to ourselves and each other in the name of ideology. You, Lord, who *are* truth and righteousness surely weep.

One man sees life as wholesale sweetness and light and dispenses salvation cheaply, requiring little, signifying nothing; it's 'grace' void of authentic relationship, absent in life-redirection, missing in any profound commitment. Good Lord, forgive.

One sees life as vengeful, a cold taskmaster, blood in the eye, *looking* for new ways to judge, condemn, sentence and execute. Mother God, forgive.

David sang how *he* was the apple of God's eye and how *Saul* was surely God's archenemy. Pardon me, God, but this is unswerving *nonsense* and David ought to have known it... there is *NONE* whom *God* despises. Not Saul, not Hitler, not skinhead, not an ISIS General, not David.

Our ideological *madness* tends toward living hells, leads toward maniacal hatreds; cripples and deforms creature and creation. Why do we kill what we do not know and like, fear and do not trust the eccentric and different? What *causes* us to become Evil's stepchildren? Do you think David didn't know this?

I am not better than David. Certainly. It's Jesus who is more whole than both of us. I am beginning, Lord, to prefer singing a different song: "Jesus loves us, this I know...."

PSALM NINETEEN
"...glory on tour...."

God, your glory shines! Your compassion pulses, its radiance *the* great light through all the *billions* of light years! Beautiful, wonderful creation! Creation ongoing! The eternal dance! Oh, praise you! Oh, praise you!

The parade of your brilliant grace *pervades* the universe, sweet Lord! The effulgence of your love-incarnate fills the stars, the earth and every soul. God's creative genius is greater far and wiser than *all* our human intelligence combined!

Praise you, Lord, whose *sovereignty* is your love! You *cannot* be completely known but, in the joy of being *your children*, your life-wonders are sparked and kindled and blazing in us! *How can it be* that you live *within* us?

Your love lives in us, its tenderizing power in-fleshed inside us. It's mystery now that inhabits the emptiness that once was within. God how is it possible that your love can heal every broken or hardened heart? Please, Lord, widen the hearts of every soul in this place today? Again I ask, How can it be that your radiant self-giving makes *whole* persons of us who were barely halves?

God's love unambiguously points to the eternal kind of life; they are a holy freedom for the once hopeless and imprisoned. God's love springs gush, quenching every thirst and leading to the greatest life of all: to *Jesus,* the holy of holies... who is for us, and *never* against us. Oh, yes! "The life-maps of God are right, showing the way to joy." Amen, forever!

PSALM TWENTY
"…everything's going to work out."

Sometimes it's hard, if not impossible to say, or see truth in, "everything's going to work out," especially if it implies "everything is going to be just fine," or "it's all coming out smoothly and well."

How could any sensitive person look around today and *not* hesitate to say, "everything's going to work out"?

God, I confess: it's for me a minor embarrassment to stand and try to *announce* a sure hope in the face of this world's realities… perhaps that's why I hesitate and humbly offer it, quietly point to it, silently cling to it: "everything's going to work out."

Doesn't it seem the lie that God rules – isn't this why only the brave or hyper announce it, blinking, bowing the soul, stuttering some?

God, when we are called to courage, make us kind, as well as bold. When stakes are high and we are confident, give us tender spirits, too. If a doubting world scoffs, put clarity and gentleness in our heads and on our lips. When the task is daunting, O God, be in us the stronger, the gentler ones, and as openly accepting toward every other as Jesus was. Let it be.

PSALM TWENTY-TWO
"My God...!?!"

Dear Eternal One, did you *really* forsake Jesus at Golgotha? Because you're the *holy, wholly* Other, did you close your eyes to him and the love he gave? Did you punish *him* for *our* sin and brokenness? If you did, I don't know you.

You are love. It's inserted permanently into creation! *We* have experienced it, we trust it, we cling to it. We are desperate for and confident in *God's love.* The *Father's* love is the love we *know* in the eyes and hands and arms and words and deeds of Jesus. Praise Creator God! That always has been and will never cease or diminish.

God-Love is prior to the beginning and will forever be. While there are they who say Jesus was abandoned by a wrathful Father, a Father who could not look at human sin and, so, the Son had to *pay* its price in order to pacify the Father, I shout, "NO!" Some would trumpet it: "It's in the Bible; I believe it and that's the end of it." Maybe, Lord... but there's more to it; there is something greater here. Read from start to finish, what my Bible says is, "GOD IS LOVE!" That's how I see it and *that's* for me the end of it.

Many thoughts are in the Bible, but the *one forever* thought is *God's love.* This one thing in life is sure: God is love and God's love didn't of a sudden back down or die at Calvary; it didn't pause even a nano-second, or hesitate at the Cross. *No,* God didn't blink; no one was forsaken there – except God (Creator, Son and Holy Spirit). The cosmic sun of grace may have been blocked by the temporary darkness of the day, but not the *love.* Love reigned at Calvary! Sovereign *LOVE!*

God's love IS! And while the Bible says, "...my God......! Why have you *dumped* me…?" God *didn't* 'dump' Jesus. God never dumps anyone – not one of God's sons or daughters.

God, it was *we* who gave *you* the pink slip. Help us!

PSALM TWENTY-TWO
"...this great gathering for worship..."

Lord of universe, heaven and earth, we shout "JOY" to the One who has never let us down, or turned away or hidden his face in our times of despising!

They who are on the hunt for God shall be found and find life abundant. God will lift the fallen and satisfy the trodden low. The straggling, confused and dizzy-of-soul will "sit at God's table" and be filled with God goodness.

Here in this gathering, the humbled bow at the feet of the valiant Prince.

We have been recovered by the life of Jesus. We have entered adoration-existence. Men from the circled globe rejoice and women from all creation break out with "Come, Lord Jesus!" – the earth is coming to its senses, hosts are running back to God, hungering for beautiful healing and rescue the Eternal Lord alone can give.

So be it, in the name of the Father, the Son and the Holy Spirit. Amen

PSALM TWENTY-TWO
"Are you as kind...?"

Are you as kind as your eyes say you are...
Are you as strong as the smile on your face...
Do you see inside us as deeply as I think you do...
Do your wounds tell both our violence and your grace?
   Ah, yes, Lord!
Do your words speak integrity and eternal truth...
Do your strong, tender arms have us in your embrace...
Are your tears a picture of God's amazing love...
Does this holy quiet say, "God is in this place?
   Ah, yes, Lord!
Will you teach us to see others with our hearts...
Will you give us your lovely hands and face...
Will you make us persons of integrity and truth...
Are the scars in *our* hands signs of your forever grace?
   Ah, yes! Ah, yes, Lord! Ah, yes! Yes, yes, Lord!

PSALM TWENTY-THREE
"My cup brims…"

I used to wonder when you'd stop loving me, Lord. If you got to know me, how long would it take? Occasionally the question still comes to mind. However, and slowly, I'm coming to see: *you love me not because of me; you love me because of you.* This, Lord, has been making a difference in me and in how I see and connect with the world. You are growing a cup of felicity and promise inside. Thank you.

Not incidentally, Jesus, this is the way I, also, want to love: not in response to the deserving of others, but because your love in me wants to come out for them. No matter what. I've been hoping lately there will come a time when I *never* judge another. I want to be discerning, but to refuse ever to judge another person. Amen

PSALM TWENTY-THREE
"...with me..."

Lord, our God: I've no idea where I'm going, or how I'll get there, or where I'll be when I arrive. But the adventure, not the arrival, matters most to me. See, Lord! I'm learning the *Holy Spirit* language. Thank you. Thank you that I'm on your way *with others*.

En route, I'll read the Word and ask some saints to teach me the ropes and moves. We're trusting *you* to know the way, believing you'll be guiding us and with us wherever we're going. In it all, through it all, you will be our sure strength, our constant advocate, our faithful pathway.

When our inner vision dims, you will be the lamp of clarity. When our minds wander or cloud over... in the midnights of our days, you are there. We cannot stumble so badly that you'll snicker or scoff or say, "Good riddance!" We cannot stray so far you'll get fed up and leave.

You're the faithful One; you've shown us this in Jesus, the Son. There's nothing we can do or become to cause you to love us less or never more. Your love, not our faith, is the resurrection, the always-life. Ours will be a great adventure, not because we are faithful to you but because you are forever faithful to us. Lord, let it be so. But, as we go, please create, also, a deep, abiding faithfulness in us to you.

PSALM TWENTY-SIX
"God, I love living with you…"
(An opening)

Set *our* eyes like flint, Lord, on all the things of God, and on the God of all things; not alone on the *life* God *gives*, but on the *God* who gives life. *Fix* our minds in the Truth and *Way* of God, but, also, on the God, who *is* both the *Way* and the Truth. Master, let us *live* not only to love, but for you, who *are* love, mercy and fire. Let this be in us, Jesus. Let this be first and center-most in us: not to *be* blessed *by* God, but to bless God and *be* God's blessers to the world. Give us to love God for *God's* sake. And let all the *people* of God say, "Amen!" I will say, let *all* the people of God say, "Amen!" Lord! God! How great and wonderful you are! Again we will say, Amen!

PSALM TWENTY-SIX
"...dancing around your altar..."

Such a depth of *mystery* you are, God! Human knowledge cannot unravel it, our wisdom cannot penetrate or encompass it, our hearts are too small to contain it. As Mary outside the empty tomb, we cannot *hold God*, or harbor and keep the wonders of God. Human thoughts, words and teachings can never climb the height, plumb the depth, discern the length, or measure the breadth of God. You are more than our minds can dream or intuit. Our greatest hymns and noblest anthems are but faint hints of the honor and glory you are.

We wonder, Holy One, is it possible to understand why you chose us to be among the bearers and evangels of your Kingdom? Mere mortals, frail creatures – we are fickle, easily distracted and somewhat scatter-brained; we cling to what we know and stick to what we already believe. We avoid, we hide from, and ignore the *impossible*. We attempt the easy, the habitual and the usual.

But, God, we adore you. We worship you. We love and praise you. We *thank* you for the few in this world who, like Mary, will say: "Here am I, the servant of the Lord. Let it be to me according to your word."

Nudge, or hasten us toward that courage, Lord. Empower us to mean what Mary said. Then, God's path will open and God's light will shine, blazing God's trail. We will dance at God's altar, rejoicing, and assisting God's children every chance we get. Hallelujah! Amen!

PSALM TWENTY-SEVEN
"Light, space, zest – that's God!"

You are the light of life, O God, the radiant source of all souls' liberty and exaltation! You are Freedom Spring, the Healing Genesis of our joy and strength. You re-birth us, equip us and empower us to live close by your side. You are exuberant, indefatigable God and in this we rejoice!

With you, Lord, drawing us together, living with and within us, no threat can undo us, we are not afraid, even the constrictions and difficulties of our days cannot harm us; life with you is full to running over. When all *hell* breaks loose, you keep us diligent and abide strongly with us until we sing again the love songs of God!

We contemplate and acclaim *your* beauty; we study how *you* act in troubling times. We want to mimic you. To abide in your house and feast on your Word are more far than owning the things our minds can crave. Knowing you love us is beyond ecstasy.

You completely *satisfy* in this consumptive world. We're in the right place now – your house – we're here to offer uncompromising gratitude. Our hearts shall whisper, "Seek the Lord," and our spirits will shout, "Oh! Yes, we shall *run* to God!" Forever together as one people, we will echo, "Take heart. Don't quit. Never, never give up! Stay with God!"

PSALM TWENTY-EIGHT
"God is not deaf."

Though we are often deaf to *you*, Lord, don't turn a deaf ear to *us*. It's a bold request, yes, but here we are, asking. Again. Keep your channels of communication with us open, we pray. What we hear a *lot* now, we confess, is silence; at times we start thinking that all *connection* between us has been interrupted, or severed and lost. Honestly, God, you sometimes seem sealed off, or ensconced in a black hole of heaven. Scripture, theology and saints tell us otherwise, but the blunt stuff of our daily living tell another story. We...aren't...hearing...you!

We *want* to hear. We *try* to hear... we listen...... at *times*, anyway. Does the silence stem from our failure to hear or notice when you *are* speaking? Is the problem that we don't hear *what* we want and *expect* and, therefore, we don't hear what you're really saying? Are we looking for clear-channel sentences and written program maps direct from heaven? Do we expect messages written in the sky, banners trailing behind God bi-planes?

Really, Lord, we know and confess: *we're* the deaf ones; our receivers don't always match your *wavelengths*. We have pet stations we prefer. Either our ears are dominantly *closed* to heaven, or they're filled with the detritus of earth-bound living? Is our inner aural nerve *healthy*? Are we hearing accurately what transpires in our daily lives, but we don't have ears for *you*? Do we *choose* to wander off and thoughtlessly tune *you* out, and listen to so much noisy world-static there's no *time* to listen for you? The world, after all, is a constant blare and your voice comes in silence, it seems, most of the time.

Renew us, dear Christ. Clear our ears to hear your voice of wisdom and truth. We know *you* hear *us*, hear our every plea or thanksgiving, query or need. We're thinking, Lord, among our deepest and greatest needs is not to *be* heard, but to hear God's voice and to obey. Amen.

PSALM TWENTY-NINE
"Bravo, God…!"

All creation praises you, Lord…Yes, all creation shouts "Bravo!" to her Creator! Angels and the heavenly hosts stand in awe before your authority, mastery and rule. The planets spin and every sun shines 800 light years around their maker. Ah! Who are we that you pay us any mind?

Hear heaven's thunder, the mighty-waters roar, and watch the tall sequoia raise holy hands! Tiniest flower stops and stands, raptly silent, firm attention, bowing, listening, quiet… silent. God's creation plays cello strings, symphonies beam, timpanies, quaking aspens, rushing streams, golden horns and glowing stars. Earthlings give acclamation, adulation, exaltation, adoration, captivation to the Lord most high! Surely, surely you are *God*! We will not forget!

Therefore, power, *all* power is God's, before whom we fall down and call, "Glory!" Glory to God! Glory to God who makes the peoples strong! Glory to God who is her people's peace! Glory to God in the highest! Power and honor and worship and love are God's, before whom all creation kneels and all the peoples bow and call out, "Glory!" Glory to the Father, the Son and to the Holy Spirit! Shouting, "Amen!"

PSALM THIRTY-ONE
"God, I'm thankful you take me seriously!"

I'm grateful, Lord, that you *trust* me with my friends. Some of them have no concern for or interest in you – and I've rarely wished *you'd zap* them, if not *clobber* them with your irresistible love. Instead, you depend on people like me to love them *for you* until *they* can't resist learning about your greater love. I hope you know what you're doing. It *seems* you're putting a lot of confidence in the likes of me. Maybe not, but it seems that way. You *do* have a way of doing that, trusting us, that is. Lord and I don't know whether to *thank* you, or be anxious. Isn't this like asking a five-year old to teach math to M.I.T. students?

Lord, perhaps I'm taking *myself* much too seriously here, and depending on *you* far too little. However, thank you for your confidence. I don't know whether to praise you, or fidget. Perhaps both? When you *depend* on *me* to assist *you*, it gets scary! You are with me, I trust. Please use me, Father, to encourage all whom I encounter and befriend to choose for you. Thank you for believing in me.

I know: it's *you*, Lord, *only* you who can bring new life to human persons. I know it's not up to *me* (I keep reminding myself). *Many* others, also, are your eager followers. Lord, keep us from fear, paralysis and procrastination. We'll give ourselves to the task. Fire us up. We're prayed up. We're ready to go… quavering.

We haven't earned "A," "B," or (probably) "C" in *Compassionate Witness 101*. But, knowing *you* trust us, we trust *ourselves* some now. Enable us, Lord, to trust you to the end and, so, we will not give up. We will persist, remembering it's *not* up to us. *Thank* you for the invitation to have a part in your Kingdom work, not of *convincing* others, but loving and serving them.

PSALM THIRTY-ONE
"What a stack of blessing..."

I've had a few dyed-in-the-wool enemies, Lord; two or three who'd "cross the street to avoid me."

They never *discarded* me like a "broken dish in the trash" ... but they didn't think I was a 'dish' worth saving. No bones about it, they despised me... disliking my innermost parts, adding bits and pieces of gossip here and there to give the abhorrence the taste of pepper and quinine.

It hurt, Lord. I couldn't do anything to make it better, or right. I could not reach them, or comfort, or converse with them. They seemed to feel sheer antagonism toward what I said and taught of biblical faith. *They* regarded it as "pastor's far-out, un-Christian ideas," aberrations in perspective and weird interpretations. They *focused* (as I recall) on matters pertaining to *our nation being one of the most warlike nations on earth;* they refused to buy *God loves homosexuals in the military and everywhere,* and *inter-racial marriages are fine with God.* Their upset confused me and I thought, perhaps I could have been more 'correct'.

Lord, I don't remember their names; I probably tried to *forget* them. Their open hostility kept me thinking at night... but I never despised them. I didn't like them. After a while, I didn't go out of my way to relate with them, but they weren't nasty monsters.

I don't complain, Lord. The bounty you are, that you've heaped in my life is so deep and high I can't see the small cluster of enemies any more. In reality, I think they helped me mature. Now, 83, I can't think of one of them. I'm not sure this is because I "worship you," as David's psalm sings, or because your "stack of blessing" overwhelms all else. You've consistently filled living with good. This stirs me with thanksgiving, laughter and joy.

PSALM THIRTY-THREE
"Three cheers for God!"

It's only right that we lift three cheers for you, Lord! That's who God's people *are*: three cheers for God! That's what we do. We let our plaudits to the Eternal rip! Were we accomplished poet-lyricists we'd write *laudacious* sonnets and great anthems to God. If we were eminent pianists our fingers would articulate the praise our souls feel. The Grands and Baby Grands would rock, the tympanis would roll and rumble, and the bass would thunder. Oh, yes! Standing ovations and eternal paeans *belong* to the Lord and God of Abraham, Mary and Paul!

Yes, we know, Lord. We know these are not the first and best of what you want from us. You don't need or want drum rolls or twenty-one gun salutes. Parades dedicated to Jesus are not uppermost on your agenda. Our hearts' adoration and thanks giving are what you most want from us… our honest praise… our souls' gratitude… *and* our joyous *self*-giving to others for you. *This* is who we can be and what we can do.

Give us vision and courage for your mission in this ruptured world, Jesus. Lord, *you'll* have to *give* or, else, we'll not have.

We know you know how much we like trumpet sounds, the acclamations of piano and drum and kazoo. So, humor us on this one once in a while, will you, Lord? Shall we dance?

PSALM THIRTY-THREE
"God is watching (over) us."

Our attitude toward you, Lord, comes from what we believe and trust you to *be*. If we trust that (in beginning) you said, "BE light!" and light *was*, we'd probably be in awe of you. That's an example.

If we're convinced that, in ancient days, your provision of clothing for our nakedness was an act of grace, we're likely to consider you *kind* and tenderly gracious.

When the psalm (verse 15) says, "He has *shaped* each person in turn…" I think it's *assuming* you have a *personal* investment in the production of every human being; *every* man and woman who ever was, is or will be is God-made. You have direct hands-on investment in creation, including every human life.

Now, *that's awesome*! That is *AWESOME*!

Thoughts wiggle and coalesce in me, Lord. First: you seek an extreme, deeply personal relationship with us. Awesome! Second is how *much* you love every man and every woman; each of us is *your* dear and beloved child. Lovely! *Third*: none, not even one, begins life *unloved* by the God of all creation. Irrepressible! *Fourth*: none of us was, is, or ever will be a *self*-made person. That's Truth. We come from you. We are yours. Amazing!

"Now he *watches everything* we do" is how the verse (15) ends. And since you shape "each person in turn," Lord, this is perhaps the most heartening promise of the psalm's many. It's not about looking over our shoulders, or forever checking up on us to make sure we're not naughty, but nice. It means you love us, you're tending us, shepherding us, watching over us day and night, twenty-four-seven. Thank you. Thank you, Lord.

PSALM THIRTY-FOUR
"A lesson in God worship"

There are times I'm not as desperate for you, Lord, as other times. Sometimes I don't feel all that needy – not at wit's end, or empty, or at the frayed terminal of my rope; the sky's *not* falling. Sometimes it's more that I'm *oblong,* as it were, out of round, so to speak, eccentric, out of balance. I don't give up on praising you; I'm just slow on the down- or up-beat. On occasion I've come down with spiritual *blahs.* I don't want to *eat* God's Word; I prefer a blander snack of Christianity-lite. I give *thanks,* but it's not mirthful or felicitous. I've had spells of living with a *slightly sour* spiritual ethos, although not a grungy one. I've had creeping church ennui. *Sometimes* my lust for *God's* life has almost slowed to a stop.

This is not to say during such times I've stopped worshiping and loving you, Lord; I *always* want to be around you and useful to you. I'm *available.* I keep showing up. I hope this is acceptable. I hope it's something up with which you'll put (that sounds really funny, doesn't it, Lord?). Right now, though, I'm not all that fired up with Kingdom verve; there's no spiritual gung-ho-ness in me at the moment.

I don't anticipate it's going to be *permanent.* It hasn't been so far. Maybe it's nothing more than a seasonal lazy streak. That's likely it. For now, I will seek you with *some* of me, some of my heart, until I have more gusto to give.

I add this, Lord: you may be okay with my situation for the time being, but it makes me a little uneasy. I prefer to be 70-100% with you and *100%, if possible.* I confess, whenever soul-doldrums creep in, or boldly attack, I start to wonder if there will be an end to them. Will 100% of me for you ever happen?

Is there something more deeply wrong here than I know? Am I insensitive to a deeper problem inside? Will there be new times of unquenchable hope and supreme confidence in God's pulsing life in me and my happy commitment? Trusting you, Lord.

PSALM THIRTY-FIVE
"Me, me, me, me"

I don't get it, Father. It 's not registering. David, it *seems*, would be shame-faced with embarrassment. But he *isn't*! His poem starts with harangue and continues with screed. From *where* does all the bravado, coupled with copious whining, come?

It's either "I" or "me" or "my" with him. Forty-three times in twenty-eight verses! "Me, me, me, me" sounds like he's practicing the notes and words of his favorite aria. "Me, me, me...my, my, my...I, I, I!"

Oh, me! Oh, my! Was David the *king* really harassed and set upon at every turn, every moment of every day, or is this a case of his presumed personal entitlement to a life of comfort and ease? Habitually he seems blind, deaf and mute to his *own* ego and behavior. Am I missing something? Am I hearing it this way *because I'm* the *same*? Are we, David and I, mirror images of one another?

I'm not in his shoes, Lord, but, perhaps he'd see life differently were he a smidgen more interested in his people than in himself! Is he here simply being a mirror image of all of us?

Father, how do you respond to our "pity parties?" Do you listen and wait, or do they wrinkle your robe? Is it *possible* *we* have the same expectations of entitlement? Could we benefit from some personal one-to-one examination, too? Although it may be a strike against me, Lord, I find it a small pleasure to discover that *David*, a man after God's own heart, had some of my own sorry traits.

PSALM THIRTY-SEVEN
"...nothing better than a generous integrity"

Father, there's nothing better in your people than generous integrity and compassionate decency. Create in *us*, we pray, the kind of *character* that's similar to yours. Don't let even an ounce of arrogance, conceit or rudeness take root, or live in us. Let not a drop of ungraciousness mar our personal profile; we never want to act as if *we've* arrived, or pretend to sit in God's favored seats.

Give us the desire to listen to others and, genuinely listening, to hear with the ears and attitudes of Jesus. If responses are needed or required, put *respectful, tender* words in our hearts and mouths. I believe it was St. Francis who said, "Be evangelists everywhere you go and, when necessary, use words."

As witnesses to Christ, we never want verbally to beat up people, or to shut down their questions, or to pound them when they don't "get it" easily. Give us patience; take all the time *you* need. Don't let us pretend to know people or their deficiencies so well that we give them our 'pet,' previously recorded answers. Your children are too precious for buffoonery. Teach us that their questions are more important than our answers, directives, or recommendations.

Make it our great desire to despise no one, especially the morally frail and addicted, and to befriend each and all whom we have the privilege to meet. Make us givers who are never stingy. Grant us forever, please, with thanksgiving to acknowledge *who* is King of the Kingdom and who the servant-workers are.

Keep ever in our minds that no one of us is so sure-footed we cannot stumble, or too nimble to fall flat on our faces. Keep your grip on us at *all* times. Hold us steady as you go.

PSALM THIRTY-SEVEN
"We've made a promise"

We've made a promise, Lord, and sealed it with you in our hearts. We have turned our backs on injustice and kicked the dark side out. It is our steeled will to work for the good and the right. We know you *love* this and our knowing it makes us want to live *more* kindly, to walk in your humility, to follow your way and do justly every day.

Like the blood coursing in us we want your Word to flow through us for others. We *don't* want to be "holy men in saffron robes, sitting in circles, contemplating the master of the universe." It's strenuous spiritual formation in Christ that makes us whole and compassionate. Toward this journey we want to keep moving and working. Plant in us *courageous* faith and authentic kindness. We seek your spacious grace, your liberating life-in-Christ, the emancipating adventure of exuberant stewardship! Amen

PSALM FORTY
"Remembering"

Gratefully I'm remembering, Lord, the time a friend standing directly beneath me, while we were ascending the same rock, placed my scrambling left foot on a solid knob of stone and, thus, made the way safe for me to clamber to the top of the cliff. In that moment, I was holding on like a tree frog to leaves, scuffing both feet and knees blindly for a place to stick one of them, and becoming increasingly out of sorts because I couldn't. The drop below was two stories. My friend casually took and moved one foot to firm toehold, as simple as that, no strain to himself, done in an eye's blink. Easy for him, but important to me. I recall that day; probably always will.

You've done the same thing, Lord, and for uncountable others in uncountable ways. I was slipping into godlessness, but you condescended, got beneath me and set my feet and life on better ground. For sure, by myself, I wouldn't have made it; *you* made sure I didn't fall into emptiness. With no footing and no prospect of attaining it, *you* were there, you were the Rock, the place to stand and you've kept me standing ever since.

Once long ago you climbed a *killing hill* and spread your arms for all humanity. That's what draws me closest to you: your deep condescension, coming to our place, getting eye-level.

The bald truth is I slide, sink, I'm incapable of completing the high cliff-climb of faith. I lose grip. Waver. But, Lord, you reach and hold me again and stand me on solid ground. Thank you for teaching me to hold on. Thank you for holding gently and surely.

You're the Foundation-Rock, Jesus, the sure footing on the journey.

I sing songs of adoration to you, Lord, and ask to be led to others, that I may help place their scuffling, scrambling feet in your toeholds.

PSALM FORTY-ONE
"An encouragement without comparison"

Lord, I don't automatically spend a *lot* of time being profoundly concerned for others. It's a matter of which I'm not proud. Lifting or *dignifying* the down and out is not my best quality. But that's your core and essence, your M-O. You '*dig*' every soul, especially the broken and oppressed. You're *drawn* to them. You don't mouth empty platitudes to or about them, or make empty promises, as I have done. Practical love is your bond and seal. Pragmatic *compassion* is who you are. It's what you *do*.

And, amazing grace, you don't look down on me, or reprimand me for how uncaring and eternally shallow *I* am toward the hungry and lost. You embrace me as your *child*, no matter what; I am cherished. Ah, Lord, *that is* encouragement without compare! Because of you I *want* to stand for others, lend a hand and give care to each man and woman whose need I can help meet. That's who *I'd* like to be. I believe that's the person you're *making* me; okay, Lord, I know the job is going too slowly.

You're re-making me, Lord; *changing* me so that I *want* to encourage lonely, hurting and searching folk, not ignore them. I want to be *large* of heart instead of small, to give myself away, instead of keeping me for myself alone.

It's not happening *real* fast, Lord, but it's working. Thank you for sticking with me.

PSALM FORTY-FOUR
"Talk about paranoia!"

Talk about paranoia, Lord! The sons of Korah have it coming out their orifices! Are they real? Is theirs the classic predicament where, even if they *are* paranoid, it doesn't mean they are *not* being talked about, picked on and ridiculed?

The sky's falling, they say, and they've "done *nothing* to deserve it." They aver never to have betrayed God's Covenant: "our hearts were never false, our feet never left your path." And *I'm* falling down crying/laughing. Who are these "sons of Korah," anyway, and I don't *want* some of what they have? I call it pomposity!

I've had people come down on *my* head, too, conspiring to get rid of me, dishing out insults and angry disapproval. I've been deeply wounded and had not earned *all* the rock throwing. But, was I perfection? I laugh out loud and cry harder.

Lord, these folk, the Korah brothers are paranoid even about their relationship with you! "*You*" (Yahweh), they accuse, "decided to make us martyrs, we wee (little lovable) lambs assigned for slaughter *each day*" [words in parenthesis are mine]. Honestly, the sons of Korah *sound* a tad more than *pathetic* to me.

If I were told *God* had decided to make me a martyr for God's cause, a lamb "assigned for sacrifice," it would raise my hackles. *God* doesn't make martyrs. God didn't coerce, command or force Jesus to choose the Cross. Martyrs (or more accurately), *witnesses* volunteer, choose, *decide* to bear witness in spite of the results that may occur. (Lord, am I getting this right?)

But, how could any one or group, including Korah's sons ever honestly suggest, much less avow they've *always* been true and faithful? Can a person ever claim perfection before God? What was the standard for these people?

Besides, isn't such talk about what I *deserve*, about never having betrayed God's Covenant and how my feet never strayed from God's path at least a few feet over the top? It's spooky to me, for sure!`

PSALM FORTY-SIX
"...a safe place to hide..."

Yours is the song of life, Lord! Lark chants it. Grasses titillate it. The trees anthem it! Stones whisper it silently! Earth wings its aria in utter and absolute praise of God – Father, Son and Living Spirit! From everlasting to everlasting you are Lord!

Toes tap to the music, feet soft-shoe the beat, our hands clap to its rhythms, souls dance with delight before the Eternal Creator! Oh, yes, Lord!

Right now, this moment our spirits step away from the busy traffic and noisy chaos into the mighty restfulness, the living encouragement of worship and the life-transforming peace of God's protecting presence.

The floods, storms and gale-winds cannot overwhelm us. Our *Lord* holds the drowning deluge in check, calms the heaving breakers and, before *God*, the storms cease. Ah, Lord God, how we do praise you; we cannot praise you as you deserve!

We dance in awe before the universal peacemaker, our God... our haven, our place of joy, our great and forever Love. Let the people who love God shout: AMEN!

PSALM FORTY-SEVEN
"Let everyone applaud God!"

Bravo, Lord, mighty in love! God most high, whose bottomless compassion softens the hardest hearts, whose passionate embrace melts and warms the hardest, *coldest* soul ... to you we carol our rhymes; before you we bow face down, hearts a-soaring and singing. We shout, "Bravo!" and "Encore!" "Don't stop!"

It's your Word, Lord, who shapes our habits, thrills our souls, molds our minds and moves our feet to bless and serve. Your incomparable *teaching* lights our way, powers our steps, equips our hands and fills our voices with thanksgiving.

Your Holy Spirit makes brothers and sisters of adversaries, creates love where enmity once dwelled, and brings hope out of despair. God crushes hatred but doesn't crush us! God *remakes* ire toward world injustice into servant actions powered by God's mercy. Praise God! Praise God from whom all blessing flows!

PSALM FORTY-EIGHT
"...a train of Hallelujahs..."

You're breathtaking, Lord! You're nearer than breath, stronger than oceans, gentler than the silent rain. You make the earth green and the mountain heights glorious with snow! The wolf howls praises to your nightlights, and flowers bloom in thankfulness for your sun. The hymns of chickadees and lark arouse our dulled ears and alert us to the songs of creation.

Send the light of Jesus into whatever darkened corners there are – in us *and* the world. Hum your melodies of grace to our wanton, wayward souls. Awaken our depths, Holy Savior, to the wonders of routine daily life, and knock us loose from soul stagnation, stagnant faith and the 'same-ole, same-ole' way of half-way fidelity.

You can do it, Lord. We know you can. For Jesus' sake and ours we ask it.

PSALM FORTY-NINE
"...no such thing as self-rescue..."

Once, Lord, such self-confidence lived and dwelled in me I was sure happiness and inner peace, success and a joyful life, fulfillment and all the right life-decisions were mine to make or build on.

When someone told me I needed "a Savior," I scoffed within (and revolted) and chuckled at one so weak and timid. I didn't know the retort, but I might have said, "There's no need for personal rescue in me, no need, whatever." If serious hazards or difficulties appeared hopeless to some, I concluded they were not sharp enough of mind, or emotionally strong enough within to overcome the barriers.

Jesus and his God were unknown to me; what's more, I didn't care to know either of them. I *pretended* to believe what some of my friends believed... because I didn't want the hassle. I was twelve when I memorized (and immediately forgot) several Bible verses to impress girls and be invited to attend, without cost, summer Bible camp. It meant nothing. I didn't listen. I could not have cared less.

I eschewed a God called *Love,* but whose own church people treated adult black folk like they were "boys" and "girls" (worse, really), called them degrading names, and wouldn't allow them on white people's front porches. It shook me deeply when a favorite African American adult carried me home on his shoulders for lunch. In response, I said to him, "Thank you, sir!" as I was taught to give thanks to others. He quickly spoke, "Son, don't never say 'thank you' to a ni....!" It hurt and confused me. I couldn't believe he said it.

Somehow I knew in (even before) that moment, even as a ten-year-old, Isa (short for Isaiah) had become convinced he was a blank, *nothing,* not a full, dignified human being, and had habitually come to repeat the awful lie. I hated "my own kind" for what we'd done. I said that day I'd never believe in mom's God, although *she*, mom, was not in the least a racist. She attended a Southern Baptist church.

One summer's day four years later, riding in a buddy's Cadillac driven by his butler, words jumped out my mouth as we five boys were talking about something: "He's just a ni....!" In that moment the word cut, slashed and shocked me. I hoped the butler hadn't heard (he kept his head straight ahead). In a situation like that, there's no such thing as self-rescue, or "pulling ones self up by ones bootstraps. The cost of rescue was beyond me!..." I was stung, stunned by myself. Of a sudden, something started to awaken in me. I began to wake up. It took six more years before I came to know the one to thank.

PSALM FIFTY-THREE
"God is dead? Or just away?"

It would be easy in our time, Lord, to despair the loss of authentic faith.

Sure, there's enough *religion* to go around and more. Hot-tub religion. Golf-cart religion. Being-alone-in-deep-woods religion. Going-to-conferences religion. Salute-the-flag religion. Consumer religion. Concert religion. Celebrity religion. *My* religion. But, *bona fide* Christ-centered faith, God-expectant, God-ready men and women who burn with God's compassionate grace-fire? The psalm suggests that even *God* has doubts about it. Where *have* all the God-consumed people *gone*? Can you find them, Lord? Are they *scarcer* than hens' teeth?

I'm serious, too, Lord. Where *are* the ones who, indeed, bend the unadulterated knee to you? David bemoans that God is hunting for *one* – just *one* – sold-out-to-God person... but God, yes, even *God* comes up empty, a basket of 'goose eggs'.

In a word, Lord, the world's going to hell in a speedboat, with hardly a soul to help you slow it down. Am I reading you (or David) on this?

The madding crowds treat you as an after-thought, *act* like you don't exist and, if you do, "Ho-Hum!" The very idea of deep commitment to you produces the shivers, while folk look for loopholes against obeying. I think it's called "*imposter*-religion."

I would despair, Lord. I *would* despair... if I didn't trust you to be the all-consuming fire of cleansing and grace, the transforming friend, the One who turns human lives toward wholeness. *I* hear the call, Lord; it's your invitation to come away from the crowd, journey life-long with Jesus and become his love-bathed, compassion-filled emissaries among the religious crowds right here and throughout the world.

PSALM FIFTY-FOUR
"God, for your sake, help me?"

So, Lord, if you'll just rip them down one side and up the other, cut off their hands and tear out their eyes, *I'll* be fine! As soon as you yank their hearts out, kill their children and dogs and *really* express *my* anger, I'll be ready "to worship, so ready." Never mind the blood.

I wonder, Father, is there no place on earth for *pacifists* (I don't mean '*passivists*'), or is humanity stuck tight-as-a-wad in mutual hatemongering and despising? Is the *anti*-war, make-peace caucus going to be relegated to beside-the-point, a *gated* ghetto in heaven?

What am I missing, Lord? David's lyrics show definite signs of sado-masochism. Why would a worshiping community *ever* sing his song? "They're out to get me, Lord, but let me de-gut them first, and then I'll give you praise, because 'you're so good'!"

The psalm leaves the impression that, since "God means nothing to David's enemies," *they* mean nothing to *God*. The only thing left to God, therefore, is to *kill* them. Wipe them out. *Annihilate*!

If there's more here than meets my eye, Lord, show me? Is this psalm clearly illustrating how self-centered and pretend-innocent we are? Does it suggest there's no other way for humanity but killing and destroying?

And why *is* it we almost *universally* see *ourselves* as the heroic, magnanimous nobility of the human race and *others* as the dastard enemy? I guess David learned early: if you're going to live by the sword, you'd better carry one and know how to use it.

Lord? There's something about justifying hatred that warps the spirit and sours the soul. That's right. And most of me wants nothing to do with it.

PSALM FIFTY-FIVE
"Who will give me wings?"

David's pain and beseeching resonate in me, Lord. I think his is the cry in *many* hearts: "Lord, are you listening?"

Biblical theology assures us God is with us; God hears and watches over us and takes care of us and more than meets our needs. That's the faith we've learned. Our teachers don't quibble, evade, or double-talk; there's no prevarication or skirting the issue: God is *love*. God is here. God is *for* us. Jesus, God's incarnation, is the guarantee. Genesis through the Revelation tells it: "You *are* listening, Lord! You hear us and are with us."

The human conundrum is not with the *theology,* but the experience. David says to God, "don't pretend you don't hear me knocking." Don't close the blinds, or go to a back room, acting like you're not home. Don't feign that you don't hear me calling your name. I see a shadow behind the curtain!

Is it the human existential experience, Lord? So we long for *Eden*? We want to believe God is near and, yes, to *feel* God's intimate love.

Much of living grinds us up, Father, tears us down, clips our wings. So much rage around us, and death! The meanness and noise deafen; the disorder and chaos suck our hearts dry. Our minds become a jumble, a churning wash and wasteland.

We've had it with the *wild*; we want a walk with Jesus on the safe side. Give us wings-in-the-wind, Lord. Come close. Let us hear you whisper our name. Please!

PSALM FIFTY-FIVE
"The hammer of betrayal"

The wounds go deep, Lord, when betrayal comes from the rage and hands of one who is the beloved and trusted. A lying shyster next door is an irritant, not a lethal dose. The departmental colleague revealing an ugly vein of bigotry, or gross, ingrained greed *disturbs*, but it doesn't kill.

But the *plotting* of child against parent, the *lies* of brother against brother, the dormant, suddenly surfacing greed within families when granddad passes away – nothing is more devastating than betrayals between kin and blood and friends. Nothing does more damage to the human heart, or kills the spirit more quickly. Betrayal among soul brothers or sisters ravages the spirit.

This is why broken *trust* is the hardest compound fracture to repair. This is why your grace is amazing. I am your betrayer, Lord; I cannot figure you out. How could you put up with me? Why would you bother when I continue to erect crosses in my head and put men there? But you, Jesus, *love* me without condition; you're exactly like the Father. Amen

I will keep working, Lord, and praying to become a true Christ-like soul for others – especially for the ones who remind me of myself. Amen. And amen!

PSALM FIFTY-FIVE
"Lord, I want, I want..."

Lord, I want many things.

I want faithfulness to bloom in your Church like the tulips of Holland in spring.

I want deep unity, dynamic spiritual development and abundant mission to rule in our church.

I want sane, wise counsel in our government, as well as noble, creative decisions.

I want our nation to put less effort into war making and much more heart into peacemaking.

Lord, I want to be a gentler, better man, husband, dad, brother and friend.

I want my thoughts, words and behaviors to look like yours.

Lord, I, also, want this: that I be continuously famished for your Word, always open to your Spirit, married to your grace, celebrating love first, middle and always, and forgiving to the utmost.

I want to *rejoice* eternally in your church to the glory of your name.

Christ is ALL!

PSALM FIFTY-SIX
"...a permanent acquaintance"

Both terms, "being *different*," and "being an *outsider*" fit me, Lord.

I remember how, at *six*, I didn't quite *fit* with my classmates? We'd gathered as a class at the funeral home. A mate had died of fever; we were honoring him. You know it all, Father, but my memory seems true: the class was given a special time, we were the only visitors, with our teacher and a few parents. A nervous *tone* layered the quiet room where Mark lay, as soft music played. *I* was fluttery inside; we all fidgeted, as we hesitantly passed by the coffin of our friend; I averted my eyes... most of us did.

When we'd "*seen*" our "*sleeping*" pal we hurried out. Immediately the first graders did what five- or six-year olds do: played. They ran and teased and chased each other around the yard. They laughed. They threw rocks down the hill, and giggled and jumped; a few boys wrestled.

But the thing made me sad. I didn't know exactly why. It just did. I was dumb; I had no specific thoughts. I sat on the redbrick stoop, wanting to be back inside with *Mark*. My classmates frolicked; I was filled with sad, 'though I didn't know what the feeling was. I felt odd, out-of-place; I didn't belong.

A lot of life for me, Lord, has been similar. I've been conscious of being sort of *different*. Not better. Years passed and I thought I was somewhat strange. For sure, different and I didn't want to be that. Occasionally I seemed *almost*, but never was *quite* in sync with others, including friends, but frequently responded to things unlike most of my peers. I was constantly somewhat *outside* the main stream. Neither *out*, nor *in*. Somewhere between, or short of, or beyond.

Lord, I've never felt *shoved* out, or excluded, or excommunicated, or like David, a prisoner. It's more like being a permanent *acquaintance* instead of a great pal, or dear friend. I don't know what to conclude, Lord. It was part of me and still is. I live with it. It's the way I am. Perhaps it will never change. I'm asking *you* to do whatever you will, including nothing at all.

Really, there are many like me in the world. And it's okay! I'm grateful for the person I am and am becoming. Thank you.

PSALM FIFTY-NINE
"Why God and David were friends"

Lord, I don't question – not a moment – how and why you and David were friends, and I don't doubt David's faith. I'm more likely to doubt mine. Time and again I've acted like the man you called your friend. I've lied, cheated, taken shortcuts because it was easy, and wanted more than my share of enough.

But frankly I don't understand David's preferred way of dealing, and especially of dealing with enemies. It seems far out of character for you, and with what I've learned about *you* through the Christ. I want to give David a lot of space; he didn't have the blessing of *knowing* Jesus. So, how have *we*, as a 'Christian' nation, or as persons behaved toward our enemies? Lord, what would *you* say to this?

I admit I've never faced local, dirty "desperadoes," the world's "hit men" and "hard cases." *David* was *hounded* daily, it seems, by men "snarling invective, drawn daggers in their teeth." If *I* were so accosted as he, perhaps *I'd* want to take such fellows "apart piece by (slow) piece," also. This is not the way of Jesus. While he *wasn't soft on sin*, he didn't look away from it, pretending our wrong deeds didn't happen.

But Jesus wasn't into *killing* his enemies; he killed the enmity. He *put himself* in their hands to show and give them (and us) *new* life. His work is always to save us from ourselves. He liberates those incarcerated by paganism. His love humbles others, rather than humiliates. They who have brought themselves as low as down could go, he brings up, sets them on their feet and frees them for selfless kindness.

We want to say clearly, Lord, trusting that you are the merciful: what David did and often *was* were contradictory to your way. *Ditto* for us. We, also, celebrate that you have baptized *us* in your love and into a new and better way, the way of *Jesus*... which *teaches* that the opportunity for godly living is upon us, and we have a *near friend* who is the same friend who loved David.

PSALM SIXTY
"You aren't giving up on us, are you, God?"

Although I don't really *know* how I'd respond or react, Lord, if my family, or church, or nation were attacked by an enemy, I want to believe I would choose to die for you rather than kill for you. I hope, anyway. I'd *prefer* that such a choice never have to be made.

You didn't kill for your Kingdom, so why would we, your followers? You gave life rather than took it. When we take lives to protect our own, whose people *are* we?

You know better than we there *are* warlike nations – our *own* being among the most prominent – and vicious tribes. But, Lord, are *your* people *ever* justified in *aping* the peoples and practices of the world, or its cultures?

It seems to this heart and head, Lord: *you refuse* to go out *with* us when we stop speaking and acting like you – which is to say, being peacemakers, serving in the great movement of grace, compassion and mercy. Perhaps you are with us, but you're being very quiet.

I don't believe there is ever a time when the followers of Jesus are supposed to act like it's time for peacemaking to *end* and for starting to make war. When, Lord, will nations, any nation, decide to choose *shalom?* Is it even possible in our time or ever to act like Jesus?

PSALM SIXTY-ONE
"Hospitality 101"

When I think of you, Lord, the word "hospitality" jumps to mind. You *are* Hospitality 101, and the clinician for *our* lifelong course in *Advanced Hospitality*. Although we may have rejected you and your care in the past, you've never retaliated, never abandoned us or turned your back on us. We've had times (aplenty) of not wanting you anywhere near us; but never have you shunned us, excommunicated us, or gotten so fed up with us you left us high and dry to fend for ourselves.

Not once have you laughed and left us to our sin, erring, or weakness. Never have you acted like we're a bad joke. Evidence of this is the acceptance and grace we receive in your church, among the people infected with your compassion. We thank you for them, the miraculous fellowship of encouragers, and for the one who are special Lights of God named "Steady Love" and "Good Faith."

In these dear kin *you* provide "breathing room," havens of joy and the "High-Rock Mountain" of hope. Therefore, Lord, let *our* days be and end as light-of-God, praise-the-Lord, love-for-others living. Amen.

PSALM SIXTY-ONE
"I'm set for life."

I've lived with and rejected many gods, Lord, but after all this time, I still let them in. Praise you, Father! Increasingly they are unwelcomed, rejected guests. They don't belong and I refuse to allow them inside my life; they're alien items who have no place in me to call their *home*. If one stops by and asks to pay rent, and I let him stay awhile (I've done it more than once), there's not an hour of genuine comfort in me. Not a minute. With *Idol* in the guest room, *I'm* uncomfortable. Another god has, on occasion, I confess, made itself right at home, even if I tried to hide him in the guestroom closet.

I'm confessing, Lord: a particular false god sometimes persists in me, hangs on, keeps coming back to re-take longer-term residence: *"Want"* is his name. I've nicknamed him, *Not Quite Enough…* not (quite) enough income, not (quite) enough dwelling place; almost, but not (quite) enough personal success. *You* know how it is with me, Lord. Most of my life I've felt *Not Quite Enough*.

I know it like I know it: *Want* is never satisfied. There's *never* enough when *Want* is present.

It's then that *More* walks in and sits.

Still… I'm thanking you! I'm praising you; you're always more than enough! It's you, Lord, who satisfy mind, body and soul. *Nothing* else can complete or make us whole.

Thank you, giving God, for more-than-I-need of life's basics. *You're* the source of every *good* thing. I'm heart-full of gratitude that you *haven't* provided everything I've wanted. Always instruct me in how to curb and defeat *Want*.

You have planted in us our deepest *hungers* – meaning and purpose and hope – and have given us yourself in whom meaning, purpose and hope are stored and given.

In you, no matter what, we're "set for life." Amen.

PSALM SIXTY-TWO
"The God of all I need"

How is it, Lord, I get my *needs* so mixed up? I confuse needs with wants. I commingle my need with my greed, my requisites with my grabby spirit.

With David, I know "everything I *need* comes from" God. God is "solid rock under my feet" and "breathing room for my soul." "My help and glory are in God – granite strength and safe-harbor God."

Lord, I *am* generally satisfied. Life. Parents. Kin. Friends. Old friends. Teachers. Life-saving educational opportunities. "Call" and work. Spouse, Carol. Great children. Wonderful grandkids. Mom's values. Good buddies over the long haul. Healthy disciplines and foods. Athletics and sports. A dad committed to his only son. Books. Brothers and sisters in the faith. Grand adventures. Home fires and family holidays. Travel. Dreams. Music and the spoken arts. Rembrandt. Jesus, Jesus, Jesus.

I try to sort out needs from wants, Lord, but it hasn't always been quick or easy. How does my yen to travel the world match up with the global impoverishment of millions and the mass starvation of hosts of children? How does my retirement at 65 with adequate income for life stack with others searching ten years for a job that 'fits' but not finding one? How does my successful study in six education institutions sit with the non-education of multitudes of young people in this country?

I've tried to share with others, Jesus, and to assist the ones I may. But, I soon remember saints Paul and Peter, Francis and Teresa, Martin King, Jr. and Dietrich Bonhoeffer and a veritable cloud of others. I've been given much and I'm thankful to the Lord and for the host of saints.

PSALM SIXTY-THREE
"We will never stop thanking you!"

The earth's springtime greenings, the summers' rains and the frozen cold of snows lingering on mountain peaks and canyon walls – these keep us alert to the shadowed mysteries of God. We will never stop thanking you for it all. Though creation can do no more than hint at the height and depth and fullness of Creator God, we will praise and bless you still, fairest One.

There's more to you than any of us can know, grasp, or imagine. We are *persuaded* that, even in heaven when we see Christ face-to-face, even *then* his countenance will shine too brightly for such clouded eyes as ours. Lord, heal and enable our seeing.

You're the bright and shining sun, the foundation rock, our source and sustenance. Thanksgiving abounds in us; it thrills in our bodies and beams more brightly than the sun in our hearts. We clap for the joy of Christ; our feet constrain us to dance. These minds will not be quelled – you wrap us in your arms; we never grow weary in your embrace. We're safe! We're hopeful and alive!

Thank you, Abba! While you hold us *dear*, you'll not let us rest endlessly in the safety of your arms; you hold us steadier than oaks in a storm, but you refuse to let us become *planted* posts. Thank you. Thank you for freeing us to become courageously your servant-men and servant-women.

What's that? It's an "Amen!" in high heaven! And a choral reading by the angels of God!

PSALM SIXTY-FOUR
"...make praise your habit."

Our desire, Lord, is to make a habit of thankful praise and worship. Our life strategy is to be molded in the shape of your Word. Our daytime dream is to look and be like the Master. We'll go for it!

Instead of whimpering when abused, we will give thanks for the growing that may come through suffering. We will use our tongues not as weapons for backstabbing, but as instruments of hope, encouragement and gratitude.

We will refuse to embarrass others in private or public, but will keep lists of the kindnesses done to us, and the kindnesses we are to do. We will live with openness and an abundance of self-giving. We will especially keep well-lighted hearts that beat for the good of others.

Of course, Lord, you know our pledge is just so much palaver unless you are its power. But when you saturate our pledge with your will, we will spread your name everywhere for as many as will to hear!

PSALM SIXTY-FIVE
"Silence is praise to you..."

We speak and we hear, Lord, in order to know who we are. Words are chief among our ways of establishing and sustaining relationship. We thank you for speech, and especially for the preaching and hearing of your Word, Jesus.

But we are *such talkers*, Lord. The more words we speak, the more we think we've said. When we've out-talked and shut someone else up, we imagine we've converted him or changed his mind with *amazing* power (it's really verbosity). The faster we talk, the quieter the other becomes. We live in an illusion: that by much talk and many words we've become great communicators.

It's a hard, if not impossible lesson to learn: the more we gab and chitchat and verbalize, the less our opportunity to think and listen; the more we hum or sing with the music, the less our time to hear, ponder and wonder.

Noise is our lifestyle: the TV is on, a CD or DVD is playing, somewhere a radio is on, the I-pod wire is stuck in our ear, the I-phone screen stares at us. If we're not cell-phoning or texting or letting the trembling airwaves entertain us, we shrink into anxiety. Quiet threatens us. Wordlessness is a menace to us. Silence for us equals void and emptiness. Lord, Lord!

Lord, give us *hearing* in our inner parts, hearing beyond words. Teach us to listen and hear with no word being spoken, and to listen with our hearts as well as our ears. Who was it who said, "Share the gospel at all times and, when necessary, use words?" Was it Francis?

Teach us how wonderful being silent before you can be, and how to obey without fanfare. Grant that our silences may become wondrous gratitude in your hearts.

The hills don't talk, yet they are alive with praise. With no single word the canyons reverberate with hallelujahs. The wheat fields are mute, but they wave to you in fecund gratitude. The wild rose speaks not nouns and verbs, but in its subtle fragrance she adores and blesses you. Each petal eventually falls to anoint the Lord with thanksgiving. The pine and oak and redwood flow with and thank our God most lovely. And we are committed to join them. Oh, let us in simple silence join them to sing!

Lord, our Lord... there are times for speech and conversation is one of your greatest gifts. Help us know when to speak and when to listen, when to preach and when to ponder, when to sing our glad Hallelujahs and when quietly to celebrate the great joy you are, when to be still and when to do. Yes.

PSALM SIXTY-SIX
"...hardscrabble country..."

Lord, I'm part of a not-so-orthodox and, perhaps, corrupted Christian coterie. Our group, probably smaller in head count than our faithful members imagine, does not believe in *post mortem* hell. We just don't - that's the nub of it. Don't know how many of us there are, but count me as one, for sure.

Our inclination is toward a hell that beats on people here and now, and in some cases long-term... We don't trust a hell where an unrepentant bootlegger burns in hell's fire forever. We simply can't believe a God like that, *especially* not the God we know in Jesus, the Christ. The God we trust could or would *never* engage in such blood-thirsty wrong.

We, also, don't have good answer to the inscrutable question, "Then, what about...?" I'm thinking of the Hitler and Mussolini, of Tojo and Stalin and the many who enslaved Africans in this country so many years? That sort. And *me*...?

Our small faction of believers is in eternal *relationship* with the Great Mystery: the one we English-speaking folk call "God" *and* the one who is the "express image" (Apostle Paul's term) of God: Jesus of Nazareth, Messiah. Some people – maybe *most* people worldwide – apparently believe there's a God who created hell and populates it with "unsaved sinners" who will be forced to roast in infinite, hot brimstone torture through all time and beyond. *Nice God.* To repeat, we do not believe this God.

God of Jesus, my faith revolves around the God of heaven, earth and eternal *life*. I have to say, our contingent puts a lot more stock in God's unconditional compassion, new-life-creating grace and unceasing love for *all* persons in all places and times.

This is my take on it, Jesus, and I hope I will always stick to it.

PSALM SIXTY-SIX
"...hardscrabble country II..."

"He trained us first, passed us like silver through refining fires, Brought us into hardscrabble country, pushed us to our very limit, road-tested us inside and out, took us to hell and back. Finally, he brought us to this well-watered place."

In our time and place, Lord, if your churched people were to *experience* first-hand this psalm's brand of training, some of us would, also, define that *training* as *veritable* hell? It's difficult for me to characterize our contemporary generations of churches as *well-seasoned, well-prepared* and *well-disciplined* by the teaching of God. David's description of 'God training' for God's Kingdom is more than likely *not* a major part of the relationship most of us have with God. *We* love concerts and uplifting sermons and scant sacrifice and lots of praise. I mean we're already overworked at work, Lord; we *do* like the dollars it brings us every month or so.

I wonder, Father, is our primary condition in church now a matter of spiritual weakness? Have we become a *soft*-covenant people, while telling ourselves we are *formidable* disciples because we attend church once in three or four Lord's Days? Is there *any* sense in which our crowd is becoming spiritual adults? Are we outgrowing the infantile and casual in our commitment to you? Are we easily fatigued by little more than the *idea* of long-lasting engagement in your name with the pagan world? Have we become distant patrons of Christian ministries and are we self-satisfied to *hire* professionals to do the harder work for us? Are we a pampered, undisciplined and mostly indifferent body in the face of God's great call to dance the dance, sing the song, walk the walk and do the vital and real work of Christ?

Have we begun to depend on others to be the *real Christians* for our time but, also, have we become *virtual* pretenders to the task? When truth is told, do we in fact prefer "the well-watered place" to all the hassle and adventure and, sometimes, the struggle of being faithful, profoundly trusting and forever committed to our God? Lord, don't answer that. Thank you.

PSALM SIXTY-SEVEN
"We've been marked!"

It's your *smile* that marks *us*, Lord! Marks us as your children. Marks us as helpers in your Kingdom. Your smile is good! There's much about *us* that could bring a frown to the brow of any parent, or bring on a permanently furrowed brow. But we have a *birthmark* and it's your *smile*. You may have shaken your head over us in disbelief at times because of our distrust and slippery faith. But, Lord, we doubt you've ever even frowned in anger because of us. We don't believe you've ever had a *split-second* of wrath.

We thank you that we're *marked* in multiple ways, Father: our *blood* is marked by our parents and their parents; our minds are marked by our expanded families, our education and culture. Our friends and habits and lovers and work have put their indelible I.D. marks on us. Of course, we've been etched profoundly by our unruly behavior and habits. But. Lord, it's *your* smile that is our birth- and eternal mark. Your *smile*!

Your *smile* is *how* you work and save and judge and care and bless! Your *Cross* is your eternal and two-thousand-year smile. Thank you, thank you, Lord. Therefore, we will honor and enjoy you forever. We, also, will someday be *all* smiles, maybe today, surely someday and then always.

PSALM SIXTY-EIGHT
"Up with God!"

Almost every time we look up we think of you, God! When we look to the heights – whenever our eyes alight on the mountains – we are reminded of you, of your power to heal and save and lift. Yes, "Up with God!"

But we refuse to follow *adoration* with "Down with God's enemies!" I'm glad Mr. Parham and mom and Aunt Ruth didn't think that of me. They kept being "up-with-God" people, trusting you to make your enemy your friend.

Thank you for Coach Cure and Pinky Lindsay and all the people of hope in my life. Thank you for being the builder of bridges. Thank you for deciding before eternity that, if walls were to be built, they'd be built by hell, not heaven.

There's a wide chasm between *righteous* and *wicked*. Frankly, the only bit of *righteous* in me is the spark *you* put there and the few sparkles inside you've been making new.

I'm *praising* you for not washing your hands of the misdirected, the wrong-thinking and wayward guilty. I'm glad "God makes homes for the homeless," and "leads prisoners to freedom," and I can't imagine heaven is happy in the least about leaving "rebels to rot in hell." But then, again, I can't imagine heaven doing that, any way.

PSALM SEVENTY
"Hurry!"

It's how I respond or, more accurately, how I *react* to the tense situations in living, Lord: "Get *on* with it. *Hurry up!*" I prefer action, not delay, not procrastination. Do it *now*. "Ready, *fire*, aim!" "Soon and very soon...!" "Yesterday, or the day before, Lord, not tomorrow!"

When I've gotten myself in jams and pickles: "Lord! hurry to get me out of this mess!" Isn't it how many of us are?

Failing to study... far too busy to do the preliminary hard work: "God! Help me ace this exam and I'll never goof off again!"

"I know I've maxed out two credit cards, Father, but if you'll show me the way out or, better, get me out, I'll be sensible the rest of my life... and please be quick about it; if there's anything I don't need right now, it's bankruptcy!"

Finding myself far from 'home' – bone weary, confused and lost, I plead: "Jesus! Show me the way to go home. I'm on the wrong road. Help me! Do it, I *humbly* ask!" "Yes, Lord! Teach me patience and do it soon!

We're not whole yet, Jesus; that truth comes to us *slowly*. But it's clear now... some things are not quick as a wink, or easy as falling off a log – they're painstakingly unhurried. We may get turned around in a flash, but maturation takes its sweet time. In a moment we may be charged up, ready to go; *spiritual formation*, however, is a life-long internship in going the same direction.

Abba, teach us long-term devotion and forever servant life. Tutor us to rejoice in delayed gratification. Instruct us in the art of *long-practiced* faithfulness. We are learning it takes more than a lifetime to love you enough.

Waiting on the *Lord* is anticipation, expectation and gravitation... not aggravation, resignation or abdication. We'd prefer it right now, but right now is not how it comes. So be it, waiting Lord. Patiently, patiently, ever so patiently, be in me. Thank you, Father.

PSALM SEVENTY-ONE
"Let my life show them you."

Father, there are times we wantonly think our firefly pin-glow can point wayward travelers to you. Forgive. What *we* need is *first* to grieve the flickering dullness of our own souls, the dark *inadequacy* within for introducing folk to you. We need to blush our fearful stumbling and panicked bumbling, our falling ever short at being *your* light among the ones whose light has darkened. Oh! God, power us to help you invite some to you, the True Light of Life.

Will we *learn*, Lord? Will we someday be your shadow-less candles burning for others? Will we become reflective images of Jesus, pointing men to you? Will your shining news take such lasting hold in us that we become symbiotic witnesses to your abundant brilliance? Father, make of *us* your light for the sons and daughters of earth. Grant us bright faithfulness, dogged perseverance and fruitful cohesiveness in the task.

Illumine the dimness in us that, in *your radiance*, you will work through us your hope and warmth and life-eternal's glow to men. God, love our brothers and sisters through *us* until grace lives brightly in *their* souls. Then glory in us all until our candles beam your starlight to the wide world. Shine, dear Jesus, until your sunup, daybreak and eternal light brighten the earth forever. Your *name* is Light.

PSALM SEVENTY-THREE
"Pretending to be what we aren't."

Lord I despise the insidious national oligarchies and vast financial duplicities in our beloved country. Politics and Big Business are fast becoming swamps of demon liars posing as humanitarian benefactors. I despise the bigotry unleashed toward whatever minority, souring the human principle of equality for all persons. Socially, we're knee-deep in plagues, especially of lies, conspiracies and dirty tricks in high places. We are beset by greedy corporations and their mogul cohorts, with cock-and-bull politicians, whom we continue to elect and admire, running the country down into a rabbit hole. Shall I ask you to forgive us, God?

The *real* contempt, Lord, is the attitude permeating populations in the country: *we have no obvious conscience or thought of repentance.* ***We can't be faulted!*** *We refuse to be faulted!* Turning from our political, corporate, military apostasy is perhaps the furthest thing from our mind. Are we but another in the long line of the once-great, but no-more? My deepest concern, Father, is: we're an epidemic of hate clubs spawned by demagogues and ideologues numbering now more than 1,700 in the 50 states. I *would like* to ask you to forgive us, Jesus, but don't we first need to deplore and turn from that of which we are part?

For whatever positive effect it may have, Lord, *I* repent my lack of open opposition toward our national sickness, and regarding my beloved country's slow demise. I ask you to forgive *us,* your church, for our passivity, our mute silence and frequent appeasement of the chaos, while the very core of our country implodes. I thank you for your great patience and grace, both with me and us. Your quiet love has been healing and helping us through it all, even as there is precious little awareness of the wrong among us that is growing. Yes.

PSALM SEVENTY-FOUR
"You *didn't* walk off and leave us."

Lord, it's a long time since you brought me home. You went to the wall for me; otherwise I was a 'goner". You 'gave it up' for me. I'd sold out to lesser gods and easier paths – and discovered late they were a little milk chocolate, but not worth a flattened penny. I believed they would satisfy, but they didn't; they *couldn't*.

Other idols slithered in when I again cracked open my door; they came in and took over… being successful, being important and well known. From a distance they had *looked* attractive but, up close, they gave off stench, like three-day-old fish. I thought I could use them as *I* willed. They had different ideas. *I* was used and became emptier than a bucket with a hole in it.

Shoving, scratching and pushing, they took most of my time and gave *nothing* of value in return. Their goal was not to assist me, but that I should fulfill *their* whims and wants.

It took too long, Lord, but, finally, the light snapped on: I was being violated, 'burned," soon to become *toast*, a burned-out case, an un-holy place, no fit dwelling for the Spirit of Christ. Losing my self, I was being pieced out and sold off in bits and pieces.

I'd been told God was real; by mom, I am sure. From my early memories she'd lived it, but I'd slammed that door shut, too.

Then, with your pestering word came a small, "say what?". With your thumb and pointy finger you pulled me softly, ever softly and there trickled cool waters to put out the fires of rebellion. The trickle patiently, painfully, tenderly, incessantly became a stream. Now it seems a long time of getting to know and trust you — but if I had a hundred years more, I could never thank you, worship you, love you or serve you adequately, or enough. That's firm.

PSALM SEVENTY-SIX
"There was a time..."

Lord, I once vowed never to allow worship to become a deadly chore, or to let your supreme gift of personal relationship slide into the commonplace. I *despise* the *thought* of taking you for granted. My confession now is, however, *I've blown it* on all counts.

I'm happy, Lord, that I disciplined myself in being faithful, but I've not always been faithful to the vow. Practicing the presence of God hasn't been easy. It *has been*, however, the most hopeful thing in my life. When I *forget* this, you continue to remind me; then I remember. Remembering is a great gift!

It's taught me the centrality of *practicing*, of working joyfully and diligently at the habit of loving you *and* loving persons *in* or *out* of my immediate life. It has brought a deep consciousness that every man, woman and child on earth desperately need you at their center, in the heart-core of their beings. Without you in every room, basement, attic, every niche of our lives, we die... before we die.

With each step on the way of this hike, march, slog, strut, dance, saunter, crawl, promenade, race and parade – the right place for *you* is our *center*. Either you *live* within us, or we will not practice your presence. Every seven and twenty-four is made for pondering your kindness, basking in your mercy, *living* in and by your light. The habit of loving *you* teaches glad obedience, kindness freely offered, sacrifice gladly given. Lord, *live* brightly in *these* lovely ones gathered here, be the head of these homes, fill every room, guide every mind and kind deed they do.

PSALM SEVENTY-SIX
"Living in one room"

I've frequently kept you in *one* room, Jesus, as if the whole *house* isn't yours. I've tried to change the locks to bar your entry. I've pretended I didn't hear you knock. I've *locked* the doors and bolted the windows more than once – you were outside, waiting. I'm not happy about it but, honestly, I sometimes become uneasy with you around *all* the time.

It wounds my heart, how I've thought and acted and grieved you, Lord. I've played at faith, *tried* to play *house* with *God*. It grieves me now.

But, Christ, there *is* something to celebrate. Steadily, and more *often* now – thank you – I want you to *own* the whole shebang… basement and attic, and all the in-between places, even the closet under the stairs. I don't want to be homeowner any more. I want you to be Master of my life. Lord, *be* the space within whom I live. Or, is it the other way 'round?

PSALM SEVENTY-SIX
"Fierce and terrifying are you, Lord!"

Lord Jesus, Christ of God: why would we *ever* think God's love is soft or can be easily discounted, is ubiquitous or undemanding, indulgent or pampering? We've *misunderstood* God, because God is unconditional love. *Why the misunderstanding?*

Because we'd *prefer* to believe your love is, after all, casual, easy to come by, not all *that* important. Not *really.* Have we understood your *mercy* to be comfortable and permissive, a bit on the furry side?

No, Lord! No! Fierce and terrifying are *you;* fierce and terrifying is your love. Your *forgiveness* is eternal; your patience is forever. You scare me. It's not your *wrath* that's overwhelms, but your *grace!* Wondrous grace! Penetrating! Unconditional!

How could anyone think God gets angry? *God's anger,* if it be *called* anger, is bathed in grief, marinated in compassion, soaked in magnanimity, replete with mercy, invaded by joy and promise. How dare we argue that God is full of "rising anger," retaliation or wrath?

You *are* fierce, dear Lord, fiercely gracious and awesomely kind. Where *would* we go but to you? There *is no* other place. Astonishing, daunting, marvelous is your life-changing amity!

A little child suddenly dashes into a busy street, ignorantly playing "fast and loose" with lethal danger. His mother screams and dashes after him. He stops, turns and is engulfed by arms that nearly crush him. "No one plays fast and loose" with love.

PSALM SEVENTY-SIX
"May we know and love you well?"

Is it possible, because of *Jesus*, Lord, we *may* know *you* very *well?* We know now you *are* and are *not* the *same* God we first meet in the First Testament, or the Second. *You are* the same and not the same God we met in Exodus, Leviticus, the Gospels of Mark, Matthew, Luke... or John, or in Paul and Peter. The *two Lords we meet are* and are *not* the same. I think.

Is the Lord God forever the mysterious Cloud of Unknowing, the mystic Creator of Universe and all life and love? Is Eternal God the forever unrevealed, or the One profoundly to know? My answer is, Yes! *Yes!*

I can tell you what I'm trusting, Lord. I lean toward wanting you in every day and hour, in my center, not merely the outskirts. I want to know you deeply enough to love you with *all I am and have*, to honor and serve you always, and never to take your love and care with so many grains of salt.

But, trying to be open about it, I can't tell if this is an honest, humble request, or an admixture of selfishness, feigned humility, with a smattering of true humility thrown in. You must judge. I *want* to be a better person than I am, but don't know if I can keep the effort going long enough in your long-term program of new construction. Perhaps I can't even *help*, not that much, any way.

PSALM SEVENTY-SIX
"...a bonfire of weapons of war."

Lord, you strike me as being *opposed* to war. In stanza one it's crystal clear: on *Zion*, the holiest of places, is where, "using arrows for kindling, (you) made a bonfire of weapons of war." The hippies of yore were not always wrong: "Make love, not war!" A professor-mentor said, "There's at least one undeniable truth about war: 'war is first and last utterly idiotic... not to mention, stupid!'"

I felt, when he said it, '*that* reminds me of Jesus.' He was a minority, a small voice crying in the wilderness. Being in class I frequently thought of the well-traveled question, "When a tree falls in the forest and no one is there to hear it, does it make a sound?" There were three or four others of us in the class who agreed with our teacher; not many more.

Once, talking with my Dad, we disagreed. Dad voiced his loyalty to country, labeling any who opposed the nation's wars, "cowards," who ought to be shipped forthwith to prison or out the country. "Love America, or leave it!" he heralded. Thankfully, for me, dad changed. I surmised it had something to do with the *draft* while I, dad's only son, became old enough to be a candidate for "Korea". Maybe it was more than that.

Lord, our nation has, since my becoming aware, had a warring madness, as well as many other idolatries pointing us to a downfall. I know *you* know the answer to our nasty proclivities, and I don't. It probably wouldn't matter if I did. Warring *is* the only god for many in power. Well, there's money, too! Warring is addiction for great numbers of anxious paranoids among us. Warring means a gigantic pile of money for millions of human beings, mostly men. But, war continues to be idiotic, as well as fundamentally stupid.

O God, Creator of the power and hope for peace, good God, forgive.

PSALM SEVENTY-EIGHT
"We're passing it along to the next generation"

Lord, what has happened in those whom your child, Tom Brokaw, christened "the greatest generation?" Surely ours has *not* been the greatest, but the *quietest*; indeed, the most quiescent... silent but not strong, except at war.

There is a *time* for silence, Abba, and for the quiet strength to go with it. But we – who were told as children to be seen, not heard – in adulthood have largely remained the mute, closed-mouth, tight-lipped generation. Our silence has *been* at times tragic, at others, cowardly – at least in part.

We *didn't* teach our children *your* Word (we wanted them to grow up with freedom to choose for themselves and ended up offering them no choices). Thus, we've had *no* word for them but our own self-invented principles. *We* failed to sow healthy seeds of truth in our offspring's fecund fields and, in consequence, God's truth lays fallow, if not dead, in their souls. Although... probably not. Maybe not. Hope not.

We *wanted* our little ones to trust God, but imagined it would come by some mysterious osmosis and unspoken nods. Thus, they and *theirs* have become flowering sagebrush rather than spiritual redwoods.

It grieves me, Lord! Oh! How it grieves! And it's getting late.

PSALM SEVENTY-EIGHT
"We don't want day-old bread!"

Lord, we're a disgruntled age; generations who are rarely, if ever, joyfully satisfied, not even with the One who is God. "More" is our middle name, "what'll-you-do-for-us-today?" our endless game. If we have enough, it's *not* enough. There's always space in the attic; we can build a shed; we can make more room.

But what *you give* is always enough, Abba! Our boundless wanting, our greedy hearts must *sadden* you; they sadden us... some... at times. You give living water; we *want* sparkling champagne. You provide the bread of life; we insist there be caviar on it. You breathe eternal life into us, but the GOOD life makes us happier. A crown, a crown... not a cross! Forgive us. Grace us. Teach us.

Put up with us longer if you will, Lord. Put up with us a little longer.

PSALM SEVENTY-EIGHT
"Listen, dear friends, to God's truth..."

How important it *is* to be a friend, Lord, true and forever... trusted, incorruptible and unequivocal; an authentic friend in speech, behavior and relationship. How *crucial* to *holy* friendship are loyalty and fidelity!

I love the hymn, "*What* a *friend* we have in Jesus!" Never has there been a friend so faithful and true as he. That's the sort of friend I want to be: trustworthy and forthcoming... without an ace up my sleeve; a person who's candid and fair, just and kind; a man who is self-giving, who never takes advantage, but gives it. Who practices one of the best ways to give – *to give in*. Someone, Lord, who loves *himself* because *you* love him, and who prefers others to himself. It's a profound thing Paul said in Philippians chapter two!

Lord, I believe this kind of friend and friendship is a centerpiece of your way, your truth and your life. Amen. Thank you.

PSALM EIGHTY-THREE
"We've *had* it with... us"

God, we're up to our ears in *self*. There's so little of you and so much of us in our living. We probably *look* like winter's tumbleweed: dry, blowing here and there, first thither, then yon on a cold and arid waste.

What do *you* see in us, Lord? Do we look like burned-over stubble after a grass fire? Do you see potential in us, or are we merely many empty promises weakly made?

We're tired of living the loose and casual life of indifferent faith; we want to be *God's* persons. Take us to your larger place, we ask. We hunger for the *high* way of discipleship. But you know it's *true*, Lord: *you* will need to do most, if not *all* the real work of soul-making. Does our *willingness* help any? You may have to light a fire under us.

By the way, we wonder if saying the above is just another excuse for not making good on our previous and habitual promises frequently made. This time let it not be so. Lord, we feel very dry.

PSALM EIGHTY-THREE
"Who says?"

Is our age so different from the writing of this ancient song, Lord? I've been hanging around your church, the Bible, spiritual books pertaining to you and scripture a long time. Taking you seriously has been the way of life for me three-quarters of my life. I've been taught the ways of God and of God's Christ by great and devoted teachers. How thankful I am! I've tried to soak up as much of the wisdom and knowledge of my mentors as I could. I have participated three-score years in the on-going adventure with the Body of Christ.

Unlike this psalmist, however, I am totally incapable of deciding who your *enemies* are. It's clear who some of our *nation's* enemies are, as it was to discern the enemies of Israel back when. But, *God's* enemies? I'm not the least bit sure.

To be straight, Lord, there probably are many who'd describe *themselves* as being no-god-whatsoever people. Would, then, *that* be reason enough to describe them as enemies of *God?*

How would one go about determining who God's enemies are? Are we not more likely to know who doesn't like *us* and who may in fact despise us than who does and doesn't like God? Is this what the psalm is doing: identifying peoples who hate *Israel* as those who, also, hate God? Is that a wise move? Clearly, we Americans would identify some of the Arab nations' as *our* enemies? Are they, therefore, enemies of *God?*

Does a man, woman or group *ever* have wisdom or spiritual vision enough to point accusing fingers at any *other* persons or groups, and conclude that they are *godless* human beings? God-haters? Is wanting and intending to kill other human beings the same as hating *God?* Isn't that a universal truth, Father? Is plotting and carrying out another's death hating *God*? Is it killing God?

Holy Spirit, I want to leave all ultimate judgments to you. What *I* want most is to discern what *God* thinks of *me* and who God wants me to *be*. So far, on both questions I've decided: God *loves* me *eternally* (as well as every person who ever lived, is now alive and will ever live) and God wants *us* to be persons so infected with *God* and God's love that other human beings see and love God because of the God-love they see in us. I'll "Amen" that!

PSALM EIGHTY-SIX
"Miserable in soul, Lord keep me safe"

Lord, someone *belonging* to you, ever thankful, praising God day and night... is the person I want to be. Make my *life* Jesus-shaped in who I am and what I do? Take the slovenly negative from my heart, I pray.

Alas, dragging my feet at the thought of bringing ultimate effort into our relationship gives me pause, Father. *My* side of living, Jesus, slows me down. How *much* of *me* must enter into living your abundant, sacrificial life? *That's* my concern, indeed, my worry – not what you *do*, but how willing I am for you to do it.

I hesitate to choose a god who troubles the waters, rocks my boat and requires *too* much of me (By the way, I'm not at all sure it *is you* requiring me to be and do anything). I want a god who under-stands serious irresoluteness, and makes allowances for hesitating personally to invest. The will in me to live as you is pathetically weak, it seems. There must be deep flaws at my core and great poverty in my soul.

Lord, "you're well-known as benevolent and forgiving, bighearted to those who need help." Well, *I need!* Will you please "listen to my cry for *help*?"

A lyric goes, "Amazing grace! How sweet the sound that saved a *wretch* like me!" That penetrates, Lord; it is descriptive, at least in my mind. God knows me like a book, sees the warts and ugliness and loves me still and all.

At my age, Lord, can you still graft *integrity* in me? Will you if I ask again? Your training in how "to walk straight," how to follow you (full of mercy), how to love justice and abide in your peace has been slow going. I need conviction, God, and nerve to go with it. I need to trust *your love* and to live as you live, in self-giving and joy… thank you for giving freely, waiting patiently and putting up with me in the meantime.

PSALM EIGHTY-NINE
"Love Song"

I sing because I'm known in heaven.
I sing as one who's free.
I sing because there's naught to fear.
I've sung since your touch marked me:
"Jesus Christ is
        risen from the dead!"

I sing unlike the cosmos,
but my song still delights your ear.
I know this because I know *you*, Lord,
and I think, to you, I'm dear.
"Jesus Christ is
        risen from the dead!"

Across the world the brothers sing
God's hymn of the faithful way.
And through the world the sisters hum
God's tune all through the day.
"Jesus Christ is
        risen from the dead!"

Like me, they lisp the wondrous words,
like me they punish the air.
Like me they sing, forever they sing
To the King of kings most fair.
"Jesus Christ is
        risen from the dead!"

(cont'd)

Men and stars and women voice
the anthem of the ages.
The song we sing is the one they sang…
the steadfast Christian sages.
"Jesus Christ is
          risen from the dead!"

The song's *your* song, our Lord and God
the song that was sung 'ere the start…
We sing it now, we sing it new
we sing it from the heart…
"Jesus Christ is
          risen from the dead!"

God's song of love is ever alive
The broken-hearted may sing it best.
How lovely is your Word dear Lord.
Your name, Eternally Blessed.
"Jesus Christ is
          risen from the dead!"

PSALM NINETY
"Teach us to live well!"

Your commands, Jesus, teach us to live well and wisely. Your directions for living authentically as your people are true and clear. We will *not* end up in a ditch or go the wrong way when we follow your righteousness-road.

The name of God is clear and true – it is, NOT ME.

The way of God is plainly marked; the direction signs are in big letters: COME THIS WAY!

And we obey. Then we don't. We fire up, then we fizzle out. It's frustrating, dear Mighty One.

Put simply, Lord, we *cannot* walk your walk, not even if you shine a bright light for our feet. We cannot follow your written instructions. We cannot stay the path we see in Jesus.

The *only* way we can live your life is if you live it inside us, our present help all the time.

Once I thought: if you lived in my core – at my very center – I'd become a robot, enslaved by your will, *bound* by your every wish. Well......yes...

I've learned more truth lately, Lord: your life is not about being a dominator, or obligator. No, it's the power of your presence inside us *liberating* us to love. It's your persuasion and finesse and generosity that convince us to yield and follow. God never oppresses, or bosses the children in God's household. Only the loved and the free live here. Maybe there are others here, also. I hope.

PSALM NINETY-ONE
"God, you're my refuge…"

This song is alive with *you*, Lord; I bow, deeply moved. How *blissful* are they who know you both in your clear presence and hidden mystery; who bow in utter reverence before your voice and *silence*. You are Sovereign God. You are eternal life! How blessed are they who, from afar, hope their King and friend is *you*! It is amazing what happens when God's mercy and grace penetrate our human lives. They who love God above all else in this world shine like *early flowers* pushing through winter snows. You are the dance of worship, the heart of servant living! You are the inconceivable presence, the eternal love.

Life-transforming love is the centerpiece of *your* character, Lord. My cluttered heart adores you.

But I confess: *my response* to you creeps along and is predominantly superficial; it has become a *painful* truth for me. As I live, teach me to be humble and honest with myself and *thankful* to you? Give strength for the long walk of becoming Christ-centered. Plant a deepening sense of your nearness in me as we go. You, Lord, who are far above and more than anything you have created, remove the many impediments in me to my faith; I don't even know them all.

I yearn to trust you sincerely, implicitly and completely; no matter *what* happens around me or to me, let me be faithful. Grant that, even when I'm dying, I will know your arms are around me and I cannot fall. *Be Lord* and *God* to me always, Sweet Jesus, until I fear nothing, except trusting you too little.

PSALM NINETY-TWO
"Look at your enemies – (not) ruined!"

It's not comfortable, Father, admitting we've been your enemy; in more ways than one, we probably still are, though not consciously or intentionally. We've been hostile to you rather than your intimate friends. What's more, sometimes we've had all the earmarks of the malevolent.

Thank you, Lord! There's another story to be told. *You* have no enemies. We keep forgetting: *we're your* friends; you've *befriended* us. We belong to you... it's not the other way around. You are the gift of hope to all, the blessing of significant and eternal living.

We admit we're often like spiritual bulls in God's china shop, the creation, slamming and crashing around. We *want* to be strong *like* bulls, yet, we want, also, to be *doing* good for *Jesus'* sake. Gentle our hearts, Lord. Tenderize our bold commitments. Energize your kind love in us. Empower your grace through us.

There's no *other* way, Lord, and no way around *it*: the only way life makes sense is *life in the strength of the Master...* in Jesus, the man of God. There may be many other ways. We know some of them. There may be a *better* way somewhere, or some day. We doubt it. In the meantime, we'll stick with Jesus and, if there's a better way, we will be satisfied to wait for it.

PSALM NINETY-FOUR
"God, put an end to evil..."

Doesn't it tear at you, Lord, that we are often brutally hard on others? That things not directly harmful to us are customarily of small concern to us? Doesn't it *crush* you that we care mostly for ourselves, *our* stuff, our narrow circle of family – rather than for *you* or really that much for your wider *community*?

Do you weep for the callousness of our spirits? Do you groan for our hard-bitten attitudes regarding the homeless, the destitute and forgotten? Yes, Lord, we *say* we care, but... As *Christians* are we not often hard-boiled, hard-nosed and heart-less toward, for instance, the unemployed?

For the dullness in our eyes, refusing to see the multitude of the lonely, Father, forgive. For the myriads of disenfranchised and poor, toward whom we mostly have blind eyes, Father, convict us. We stand by as the wicked get away with murder. Change us, transform us, Jesus. We point accusing *fingers* at the greedy injustice of the mighty while, at the same time, we find reasons to be complacent, or complicit and silent, ourselves.

Install and instill compassion in our souls, dear Christ. Forgive, and *empower* us to love our brothers, every one, and to *do* your justice and mercy where we live.

And, Lord, there's hardly any point in asking *you* to forgive us if we have no intention of becoming *like* you, our Teacher, who forgives *our* every fault and sin? Don't let us be satisfied with being forgiven.

PSALM NINETY-FOUR
"A confession"

Lord, with perhaps *many* of your followers, I don't need you to be a haven of rest for me right now, or a safe sanctuary from the world. I and perhaps others are not all *that* sold out to you... to your lionhearted daring, valorous courage, or condition-less love.

As I look in my heart, Lord, I see glaring absences and imbalances: not being a consistent help for those in trouble, for example, or a man serving the hungry. I hardly minister at all as a skilled spiritual chauffeur for the spiritually crushed, or a good housekeeper for messed-up lives. I don't yet feel all that comfortable living as one of your reflective lights in the darkness of the world.

I have retreated from too many opportunities to be like *Jesus* in the world. Many have been the times I've used God as a *hideout*, rather than a resting place. I don't need *rest*; I need to be useful. Most of the time I'm just running: in circles, to keep up with my neighbor, or running away from the long commitment of following you.

But of this I am confident, Lord: you changed Abraham, Joseph, Peter and Paul. You surely are capable of changing me. Will you, also, Lord, make me willing to *be* changed?

PSALM NINETY-SIX
"Sing!"

Yours is a "terrible beauty," Lord – exquisite grace, immeasurable truth, a scintillating love more penetrating than the sun! We are happy to sing our fertile adoration to you, to your beauty alone!

How, O God? How shall we "shout the news of (your) victory" when *you* don't live in us? Shall we take the story of God's goodness to "one and all," if *we* have refused to live and celebrate it, ourselves?

Our deeds, good Lord, are a house-of-cards, collapsed by a wisp. The slightest gust of criticism blows us over, or down and evil-fear comes rushing to dig in and stay a while. Your scrutiny unravels us, Abba, *not* because you are to be dreaded, but because you *are love*, and to *be* loved.

Our faith is whisper thin, our word but shallow promises hastily made, broken in a moment. Our gods look cheap even to us, but we keep and closet them, just in case – they are rags, you are riches; they are twigs, you are the Tree of Life.

You are exquisite, unfathomable, immeasurable, inestimable, unspeakable – our petty little gods are nice, soft, cuddly, self-made, thread-bare teddy bears. They command not, they have no reality. They are nothing.

God is I AM, the Lord most high, the Bravo, worthy of ten-thousand hallelujahs. The Lord's "terrible beauty makes the gods look cheap," cheap *and* beside the point. Redundant. To you, Lord, to you *only* shall we sing and bow! You alone we will serve! Help us!

305

PSALM NINETY-SEVEN
"God rules..."

Father, looking at the world, it's clear the wealthy and the mighty rule. This earthly home seems an unholy glut of powerful oppressors, the playground of the dominant who think their prominence will never end.

You rule, Lord. We are learning it: *you* rule, God of love! No matter how our faulty eyes see, you are sovereign love and will not fail. Never mind the domineering corporate powers; they are pip-squeaks. We will not pay undue *heed* to the greatest military force the world has ever known, or to the impertinent militants and governments of men. No. We are taking an alternate route: yours.

It's YOU, O Lord, who presides over creation. You're master of the universe. Our manufactured, neon, hand-made gods of greed and pride and pomp and fad and celebrity may try to stand beside you, but they *melt* like snowmen under a summer sun.

Our eyes have *seen* your coming. Our minds are illumined by your Love-Light. Our hearts throb to the eternal music of your voice. It's *all* about your grace and excellence, Lord, about your Word of truth and life.

You are God, *the* Lord God Almighty. All else, by comparison, is arrogant fetid air, pretentious absurdity, a preposterous silliness. We will not be deceived. Neither will we waiver nor hesitate to trust you. We choose *you*, indeed, as our way, truth and life. God *rules!*

PSALM NINETY-SEVEN
"Ragamuffin gods"

How silly, preposterous and laughable I am, Lord! With permanent blush I confess: I'm your twit and half-wit. With others of *humankind,* I'm no simpleton – but, in *your* presence, I'm a blockhead, a bonehead, one of God's beloved hardheads.

Abba, this is my ardent confession; so, why does it sound almost laughable? I *am permanently* an idolater. I've sensed myself to be one of the devil's henchman. But you *know* it's not what I *want* to be.

You know me well, Jesus. You know this confession is only part of the truth of me. Nothing is hidden from *your* eyes. Your insight nails me epicenter. Your truth penetrates the core.

There's more of you to be spoken, Lord. If I could decipher it, or comprehend it, even then I could not *say* it well or true enough. I believe you take me and all humanity – including our "ragamuffin gods" – seriously, with forgiving, gracious kindness.

I believe, also, and even more deeply so, your *love* is primal and never ceases. Why, then, would any of your children *not* chuckle at ourselves *and* our "ragamuffin gods"? And why would we not love you and your Kingdom Way with resplendent joy?

PSALM NINETY-EIGHT
"God's love, en-fleshed, let us be"

Lord, you *create* in love and, though your creation is inexpressibly wondrous, *we* have *compromised* it; creation, in our hands has become abused and tainted. We were created in love to love; made to be caring grounds keepers, wise garden *stewards*, but we have been spoilers, poisoning what we touch. Forgive us. Grant that we may repent.

We're *amazed* you continue to love us, Lord, although not really. Your indwelling love bewilders and stuns us. Beyond rhyme, reason, or religion, you *hold* us, you hold us dear and *near*. You wrap us in your arms and enfold us. You become one *with* us. How could it be?

How can it be, Lord? God's love en-fleshed, then re-fleshed in *us*? Could it happen? God's love *in us*, *loving* others? *Amazing* love! Lord, let it *be* true *in us*. Let us be like earth, providing food; like deep springs, giving bountiful, sweet, refreshing waters; let us be like sun, shining, reflecting the light of Christ for darkened eyes to see. O, may your stumbling, needful children see a God-path in us. *Let* us, your church, be *Bibles*, ministering God's Word of hope.

In *these moments*, Jesus, in this worship, let us be like ocean breakers, roaring our applause toward you; like philharmonia, let us fill this place with God-song, joining as we *do* with every living thing to worship and laud you, Creator-Savior and God. Amen.

PSALM NINETY-NINE
"And they did what he said..."

I don't know what it is about me, Lord. I see good all around and give thanks to the Most High. The works and deeds accomplished by your human creatures are numberless and there is every reason to be filled with gratitude. And I am. It is good. You provide. Past and present, our brothers and sisters of all lands and nations have done great things. I say, "Let there be thanksgivings all around!"

Why, then, is it, God, I frequently mention in my prayers and even harp on human *faults*, wrong doings, right actions left undone? Why do I point out our human practical atheisms, our national murderous actions (called 'wars')? It's depressing to shame our greed, adultery, brutality, racism, misogyny, nationalism and abuse of the poor all the time! Why not emphasize our good qualities and positive actions more of the time?

Sweet Lord, is it because I haven't yet figured out our true core as human creatures and spiritual beings? I don't think we're mostly *bad*... not at all. Created, if we are, in your own image, it makes sense that we would be mostly *good* and potentially godly. Have I mistakenly interpreted human *immaturity* and called it *being bad*? I certainly do not equate sinning with being evil to the core! The optimist says, "This is the best of all possible worlds." The pessimist responds, "It's a sad thing to know you are right!" I seem to be stuck somewhere, between about 45% positive and 55% toward the ugly parts of humanity. Perhaps it's part of being an agnostic as long as I can remember.

At this stage of life I lean more to the side of *sin* being a matter of childishness, natural self-conservation and immaturity than our being constitutional wrongdoers. Our *natural* way is to love and obey Eternal God our Redeemer. It is *unnatural* to be self-centered, mean of spirit, abusive, ugly towards others. Nevertheless, we *can* be mean as snakes and poisonous creatures. Lord, save us to our real selves. Thank you.

PSALM ONE-HUNDRED
"...we didn't make him"

Lord, I've conceded, acknowledged, openly admitted, repented and testified that there's a skunk in me, a turtle in me, a jackal in me and an artful fox in me. In a crisis, I spray. When seriously confronted, I retreat. If attacked, I get more than mad; I get even. When needy, I scheme. I've wondered occasionally if that's what I've mostly *been* and really am.

There's, also, a poet in me, trying to speak to God's beauty, and a song in me, wanting to be hummed in joyfulness. There's a priest in me, eager to listen and hear and serve. Yes, and there's a heart-for-God in me, although, often, it is not beating with the rhythms of the Master.

There's a workhorse in me, ready at least half the time to help pull the load of those weighed down with troubles and fears.

And, Abba God, there's *the* Physician in me (Jesus); He "is sheer beauty." Eternal grace.

PSALM ONE-HUNDRED TWO
"Hurry, Lord!"

God: you save and make new! My spirit **thirsts** for you and the new life you give – not because I'm in any way saintly, but because I am not. I yearn to be more present to you, more available for you and more usable in the mission of Jesus.

Perhaps many find it (nearly) natural to receive and then return your love, and to follow you faithfully with glad spirits. But I – and I imagine there are others – am *desperate* for you.

At times in the journey I thought my need for God was fractional. No longer, Jesus. Perhaps it's just part of getting older. I like to **think** I'm just getting wiser, but I honestly doubt **that**, too, Lord.

For me now, and others (I'm sure), our need **remains** "desperate." We ache for you and your radiant and pregnant way. We're urgent for you, in a hurry for you; not **panicked** … **urgent**.

My need is not to be a **little better**. That's no longer a concern. It's not a few gentle nudges along the way for which I'm starving. Most others may not see me (us) as a parched **wasteland**, but they can't *see* me (us).

Some of us, Jesus, are dry and barren souls, but you know that already; no, there's terminal illness both in blood, bone and soul. We will die, all of us, yes, but without *you* we are living dead.

I'm thankful, Father, there are salt-of-the-earth folk, your **holy** people; I'm amazed at seeing them live and, yes, I'm envious. I don't resent that you (may) have chosen, called and anointed some to bring God's life-spice and sustenance to others, and to minister it with élan, poise and effectiveness.

Come, Lord, into whatever I am. Come now. Bathe me clean. I don't know how much cleansing power it will require. I'm not sure it will do much good. I *am* quite sure, though, that you are the one for the job. If I'm ready, if the time is right, do it. Let it be.

PSALM ONE-HUNDRED THREE
The Lord "keeps in mind that we're made of mud."

Like the trees of the forest and bison on the plain, we came from dust and to dust we will return. But, holy one, keep our minds and spirits **out** of the **dirt**. Give us integrity of mind, honesty of heart, genuineness of life. Put your self *in* us that we may walk by your truth and love as you love.

Living as most of us do in the lap of easy luxury, we find it convenient to live without you; and **almost** as easy to live without others. But **that's** the centerpiece of sin, Abba. We know it. Living without you and others is **not** life. Our hearts are empty if you're not our source and strength. Our **lives** are nothing (but egoism) without communities of sisters and brothers, the vital families of God.

We have but few years here on earth, Lord. Without you and communities with us, we are like wildflowers springing up and blossoming; then we disappear. Gone in a moment. Holy Lord, teach us not only to *count* our days but, especially, to make each of our days count for you.

Establish permanently within us the undying quest to live for you each moment and to **bless** you by blessing **others** in your name.

PSALM ONE-HUNDRED FIVE
"...sold as a slave..."

Like Joseph of long-sleeves, Lord, we've been brats – self-centered, imagining that your blessing is our personal right and entitlement, rather than your summons to responsibility. We've thought God's first and final purpose is to pile on us God's endless goodies, favors and advantages.

Unlike Joseph, Father, **we** – finding ourselves up against walls and in tight spots, experiencing unfair treatment from those we love and unjust treatment at the hands of those we hardly know – we whimper and cry, "Foul!" We growl and 'beef' at high heaven about road-blocks that hinder our progress or slow down our getting what we think we deserve and want – right *now*!

Lord, we want success without suffering, worship without work, peace without its making, inner strength without discipline and joy without personal commitment.

Toughen us up, Abba, that – in the face of any opposition – we may be filled with your grace and running over with your mercy. Strengthen our determination and 'steel' our wills that we may not flinch from your work or shrink from living your love. Teach us that your compassion is wear-and-tear resistant, as durable as leather, and muscular in its kindness.

What you did with Joseph of old, Father, firms our persistence; it guards us against stumbling and settles our fears. We are ready. You are able. Lets keep going on the Jesus-road. Yes, indeed.

PSALM ONE-HUNDRED SIX
"...your celebrating nation..."

Yes! Oh, yes! The Lord God is our Hallelujah Joy!

God *is* love and God's love *lasts*, never wanes or comes to nothing. God's Love, *Jesus*, doesn't melt in the heat of conflict, or crumble under pressure. God's love is unchecked and irresistible, and he *is* our saving grace!

Why do we thank God? Because we cannot thank God *enough*; because our thanksgiving is ever small and inadequate. We *keep* thanking God because gratitude is the best we have to offer.

We may give half our goods to house the homeless, feed the hungry, clothe the naked, care for the sick, love the orphaned and bear witness to Jesus. But without responsive *love* and *thanksgiving*, we're just doing our duty.

We sing "Allelu!" because we are speechless before God's love. A genuine "thank-you" is never enough, but it's our highest return. Thank you! Thank you, Lord!

Most of the time these days, Lord, the peoples of this nation it seems are angry, at each other's throats. This is surely hyperbole, Father, but in my eyes it's really looks bad, and is becoming worse.

Occasionally, however, small things come together and the ***nation*** lifts thankful hands: a Caucasian college baseball coach donates a kidney to an African-American-freshman baseball player because, "It was the right thing to do."

Nothing, not even "Thanks!" can touch such love. O wouldn't we enjoy seeing and hearing a lot more of that!

PSALM ONE-HUNDRED SIX
"After all that much time…"

Lord God, I don't think I've ever recognized it or, perhaps, I've never been fully cognizant that "They sacrificed their sons and daughters at the altars of demon gods. They slit the throats of their babies… the blood of their babies stained the land."

I am stunned to silence! After all these years, it never dawned! How could it be? Hundreds of years passed between Abraham and Moses and the life of Israel in Promised Land! "They slit the throats of their babies?" **No**! Abraham was born in and came from a 'world' where child sacrifice was almost universally practiced. However, Abraham learned the clear and firm God-message that sacrificing ones child and other human beings to ones god is idiotic.

I'm at complete loss, Lord! I didn't know God's chosen ever stooped so low – not after Abraham and Sarah! But… then… again… Lord! It's not far from murdering children – never mind their parents – called Philistines, Amorites and Vietnamese to sacrificing ones own offspring… not if you're desperate, or afraid, or feeling entitled.

I'll leave it at that, Father. I am speechless, sad and disenchanted. Then… again… Nagasaki, Hiroshima, Guernica, Dow Chemical and a man named Anglin come to mind. Or, am I imagining my gossip, rage and character assassination are all right with God?

"Blessed be God, Israel's God!
Bless now, bless always!
Oh! Let everyone say Amen!"

PSALM ONE-HUNDRED SEVEN
"Sing it out!"

At last, Lord: we are not afraid of the open ocean, existence, or of the unsettled seas of daily life! We are not afraid of living with you because we...

"...thank God for his marvelous love, (and) his miracle mercy to the children he loves; He shattered the heavy jailhouse doors, he snapped the prison bars like matchsticks!" We are no longer afraid.

At last we can sing out! We are liberated! We see the beautiful light! Finally our lives are bathed in God's life and dynamism! Marvelous love, miracle mercy, astonishing grace!

Our highest praise cannot touch God's deserving. The Word was spoken; now grant that we never mistrust it, defy it or deny it. Put truth eternally in us and provide that we live it with open heart, blithe spirit and free commitment.

Then we, too, will be your people of the promise. Amen.

PSALM ONE-HUNDRED NINE
"Send the Evil One...?"

Are we of this new century so *different* from David, Lord? David talks himself up and his enemies down. Are we a fraction of an iota improvement on that? Do we not shout "Praise God!" one breath and the next breathe hate, invective and judgment? There's no getting around it, Abba Lord: we "Hallelujah" you then wash our hands of the hatred stalking the nation.

We pray for peace and vote for war, and we seem to care not that people die on killing fields from bombs *we* manufacture and drop, and sell to other nations who use them to kill our *own* young men and women.

We plead that God will visit God's embattled world with healing; but proceed to put on innocence masks, twiddle our thumbs, sit back and say, "We're not responsible; what do we care?" One could imagine the "Evil One" has us in its grasp. **But, we refuse to take this for our answer**.

You can deliver us, Lord. If it's to happen, you must deliver us from the messes we make and re-create us your new creations. You can put in us the mind and spirit of Jesus. Then our hearts will over-run with peacemaking, and our legs will move bravely to serve the ones in need. Trusting in you, we will cheer and sing our wholehearted praises to the Lord our God! By the mercy of Jesus, we shall walk his walk.

PSALM ONE-HUNDRED TEN
"Sit alongside me..."

O Lord, our God... we have no throne rooms except our hearts; no chandeliers, no gold adornment, but we are your royal household. We aren't kings... we are your servant priests. You have anointed us with full shalom. In our weakness, we cannot walk or serve as co-laborers with you, or take equal shares in the work you do. Yet, you never stop being our strength, our confidant and lifebuoy and we will love and serve you always.

We aren't equals, but you treat us as precious friends. We're barely on your side, even if we imagine we are fully there; still you're at **our** side, not necessarily with blanket approval; you're forever our forgiving love. You're for us, your hand of anointing is upon us. You always have our backs.

Lord, "enemy" is a man-made attitude and word. I doubt you've ever uttered it, or experienced it. You choose no sides, but are for all sides. You have no favorites... amazingly you favor all humankind. So, Lord, when we label a neighbor as "enemy," we're not your friends... nevertheless, you're ours. You remain. I believe our "having enemies" breaks your heart. I pray you will hold us and teach us, as well as correct us until our hearts become as yours.

More than anything, Jesus, our main mission is not **to be** loved, praised and served, but to love, praise and serve you by being servants to the wide, wide household of God. Do it in us, through us, with us, Lord. Thank you.

PSALM ONE-HUNDRED TWELVE
"Blessed man, blessed woman, who fear God…"

Truly, surely there are wicked men and women in the world, dear Jesus. I am one of them, without you. Without you, a wandering emptiness pretending to be whole inside. The hope in me is your gift. The dim candle of generosity inside twinkles because your sunburst of lavish beneficence lit my soul. Your light has risen in me, a great surprise at the start. How, Lord, could your shine penetrate this resistant heart? How did you make this heart ready to trust you? How did you convince this cynic of your presence? How did you melt the icy doubt? How did you replace my agnosticism with trust?

Your self-giving never runs dry or out. Your ready-grace keeps shining like the stars. I will forever cherish the overflowing depths of your love.

PSALM ONE-HUNDRED TWELVE
"About whom are we talking?"

I don't know many like this, Lord? I know some who seem to "cherish and relish" your commands, some whose "houses brim with wealth" and some whose children are wonderful, robust and wiser than their years. I know a few in and out of whom sunshine lives, even in the darkest of times; that's how they present themselves in church and public, anyway. I know a man in Cleveland who returns 90% of his income to God's church and lives on $62,000 a year in a family of six. Some there are who, if they're telling the truth about themselves, are "unfazed by rumor and gossip, heart ready, trusting in God."

But, Strong Mother, I don't know a single person who combines all the good qualities and characteristics here named. It's as if we meet here someone tantamount with Jesus: "Upright" and "blessed," for sure. "A generosity that never runs dry," oh, yes! "God's grace and mercy and justice!" indeed, enfleshed! "An honored life! A beautiful life!" There's hardly a better way of describing him.

What I like most about this encouraging song, Father, is there's no heavy obligation, or pressure, no compulsion, severe onus or coercion in it. I don't see should or ought or have to or must anywhere. Here are a "blessed man" and "blessed woman" who fear God and love God's road map. No nervous "shuffling or stumbling around" with them, no fidgeting or nervous tics.

I want to make a copy, frame it and hang it prominently on the wall where, when I get up each morning, it'll be right in front of me. I'll probably not do that, Lord. For some reason, I've come to distrust posted placards. But, I'd like to remember to read Psalm 112 every once in a while. Thank you, Lord. You're good!

PSALM ONE-HUNDRED THIRTEEN
"God is higher than anything..."

Thank you for the mysteries and the unknown, Jesus, for the incomparable and unfathomable. Thank you for the hints and nuances and glimpses of you, the ever-so-slight sightings of you throughout our lives. Thank you for the hidden and concealed. Thank you for the veiled and ineffable.

You are incomprehensible, O God, yet you are incontrovertibly here. You are inconceivable, yet always present and near. And bless you, Lord, for the *Great* Surprise: your good Word who lives and is with us forever.

How excellent is your name, O Lord! How *excellent* is your name!

PSALM ONE-HUNDRED FOURTEEN
"Sea took one look and ran..."

Lord, I know you don't turn the oceans' tides with your hand; it's not your vocal cords that thunder; an electric storm isn't your glory cleaving the sky.

You *can* mend broken hearts; this I do not doubt. You can *lift* a man from the muck and mire of self-destructiveness. It's clear you often restore shattered lives and disintegrated relationships.

Then, why do I hesitate to believe you brought drinking water out of solid rock? Why do I find it hard to say you parted the sea and let the Hebrews cross on dry ground to the other (safe) side?

How is it, Lord, I'm a skeptic about the Jordan River stopping in its tracks so the people could cross over into Judah – when I *accept* as *fact* and truth your healing of Jairus' daughter and the raising of Lazarus from his grave?

It troubles me. Have I become immune to your sovereign control in the world? Have *we*? Having come to accept evolution as part of how God works, have I stopped believing in the God *who* works miracles? Lord, your creation is miraculous. Do I *continue* to trust that the Lord God is creative, and that our eternal human need of God's re-creation will remain forever?

My answer, Lord? No, I have not become immune to miracles or a cynic who scoffs. Trusting you is the only thing that makes good sense to me. Jesus, thank you for the continuing work you're doing in me.

PSALM ONE-HUNDRED SIXTEEN
"...because he listened..."

Jesus, I wish there were no limit to my confidence in you. How wonderful it would be to be filled constantly with your peace, balance and love. Were I replete to the brim with your insight, wisdom and passion-for-good, I would be one of your shining lights for others in your kingdom movement.

Come to think of it, if that were the case, I'd have very little need for you, Lord. I'd be imagining all sorts of vainglorious lies about myself.

It's perfect the way it *is*, Father, even though *I* am a far, far distance from perfect. I love *you* **because** *you* love me. That's the way it is and needs to be. Your love came first, mine came in response. That's *your* way, and your way is good. Of course, before the Word came to us, many human beings loved you... except they didn't know you and had myriad visions of who you are.

We love you because you came to us. We love you because you don't need our love in return. Oddly, *that's* how we may love you best: when ours is response, welling up freely from within; ours comes not from obligation or duty, but in thankful response and grateful love. If *ours* were *perfect* love, we'd *choose* to love *you* whether or not you'd love us back. We are incapable of doing that.

Our love, Jesus, if founded, created and sourced by your eternal, unquenchable commitment and loyalty to us. We cry for mercy, then discover it was *always* within us. When we *call* we learn you've been listening the whole time. When we're stretched too far and don't know what to do, and forgotten where to turn, you've been holding us in your arms from the start.

Lord, our love for you is partial and impure; it's that way, as well, as for our fellow human beings; but we rejoice in the incredible gift of *knowing* that. You, O God – your attentive and never-faltering grace – make us glad. Teach us, also, to know the need we have for our most precious ones, our neighbors and friends and for the peoples of this world. Let it be so.

PSALM ONE-HUNDRED EIGHTEEN
"Say, 'Amen'!"

The people of God say, "Amen!" When the tide was against the Hebrew children, God reversed the winds and waters and God's children passed over. The floods of struggle have often threatened the faithful ones of Jesus. But, we will do more than shout praises; we will *live* God's praise. God-songs will be in our walk, our will, our work, our ways. We will not forget or falter. Putting aside every difference that could separate or alienate us, we will move as one body in Christ, our one heart beating by his power. His mind is in us making God's good life, salvation and mercy *known* to our God-loved neighbors.

Our *voices* are for whispering, lisping, singing, proclaiming and shouting God's life... that God's life may come to many. Our hands are for jubilant giving... that none may have need. Our legs are for climbing the mount of *our* transfiguration, leading us to be as he was. Our feet are for walking the way, the truth and the life after him, our Lord and Teacher, Jesus. Say, "Amen! And Praise the Lord!" Right on!

PSALM ONE-HUNDRED EIGHTEEN
"...trust in people..."

Knowing a little of my fickleness, Lord, I figure other people can't always be counted on, either. Many are the instances I've said, Yes and meant, No. I've made lots of promises I could not or did not keep. Some promises, in younger days, I didn't intend to keep. Fickleness! Nothing I can think of has caused me more personal regret, or a deeper sense of doing someone a harmful wrong, or of having failed.

Practically everyone who has ever known me well and been a longtime friend has commented that my trusting comes too easily and soon. "You're so naïve," they say. "Some cheat is going to take you for a ride, financial or otherwise, someday." Well...twice it's happened.

It's not fun to be fooled. As a ten-year old, several older boys played a variation of the "snipe-hunting" trick on me. They stationed me downstream in a narrow creek with a seine in my hand and told me to wait while they went upstream and scared the fish coming downstream into the net. Probably along with many, I've been outwitted, deceived, betrayed and made a sucker. I didn't like it, although I knew the guys in the creek were having fun. I've been baited, mislead and defrauded. In consequence, I know myself well enough, Master, to know others fairly well, too, and, therefore, I know now not to trust everyone.

Admittedly, Lord, I continue to be naïve. What does it say about me that I'd prefer to be the brunt than the hammer? I'd choose to be neither. If it comes to one or the other, let me be the brunt.

What scripture says I find to be more than often true: "Far better to take refuge in God than trust in people..." I don't doubt it a second. You, Lord, **can** be trusted, although I admit trusting you didn't come quickly for me, except by the proverbial two-by-four method. It was easier to trust the men and women close to me in my life, and a few friends whom I could see and live near than to trust you, whom I could neither see nor hear, and with whom I never spoke.

But, Jesus, I've come to believe it was in trusting some others implicitly (I decided and chose to do so) I came to trust you. It seems the psalmist's declaration is largely true, but it doesn't always hold. We can trust some people, I suggest, with our lives. They can't provide everything we need, but we can trust they will try always to be true, kind and forthright.

PSALM ONE-HUNDRED NINETEEN
"...a stranger in these parts"

This is probably a strange conversation, God. There are occasions and I cannot predict them, when something happens and it seems prayerful, but it's not exactly praying. I hardly ever talk about it and I don't know how to speak about it fully, or even half-fully. At times, Father, I experience a near, almost direct closeness with you – so close it seems like I'm a little child in the arms of my mother, or with a master teacher who patiently listens to my lingering questions. You're more real than I am when the experience comes. It doesn't come often, to speak honestly. Truth be told, Lord, I'd like it to be more frequent, but I'm not sure I could take it if it were. Sometimes it feels I'm almost one with Jesus, dear to Jesus; I can almost touch him. It's like being embraced by kindness, or an awareness of the sacredness of a place, or when an 'ancient soul' is near. During such moments, when I am intently aware, Lord, I usually don't want to move, or stir, or even think. I want to stay right there. Without fail, however, and I don't know how long it is, the word of Jesus comes: "Follow me and I will make you..." (it's a sort of mantra for me). Most often I am reminded to 'feed the children and care about the old ones.' Something real that I can do. I'm usually a little nervous, or excited and, later, I am thankful, filled with gratitude.

PSALM ONE-HUNDRED NINETEEN
"Talking in our sleep"
(verses 65-72)

You've taught us the Bible is good, Lord; it is good, true words, but it is not the Word, not God's LIVING Word. The Living Word has always been with us, before Eve and Adam, in our midst forever... loving and giving life. He lives among us and indwells us now. Amen. The Bible, for us, Lord, is your words written by men about the Word who is eternal. Praise you, God! Your Word is beauty, sustenance and life.

Lord, teach us to know and celebrate: that our words about your Word are never the Word; our words will always be less than your Word – inadequate, shallow, out of their depth. But, thank you, Lord: the words we speak about the Word you speak can be worthy and effective... when your blessing is on them. We bow before you to ask.

Let our basic training in living start with this, Jesus: it is better to dance with you, the Word and to sing your Music than wander through life talking in our sleep. Your Word is measureless Joy and the Drama of life. There's no other word for us.

God, will you cover our feeble stuttering in your name with love's thunder, and back-fill our hollow jabber with your eternal Self. Use the baby talk of your people for your eternal Kingdom's purposes. We know you will. Thank you.

PSALM ONE-HUNDRED NINETEEN
"No 'fast food' here"
(verses 97–104)

God eternal, I was twenty-two years old when, one Sunday afternoon in a North Carolina Baptist meeting house, my grandfather, his bulky hands on my head, quietly said to me, "Son, from now on you must eat the Word." I'm reminding myself, Lord; I know you remember.

I'd no idea what he meant, except for noticing an instant sense of warmth inside... I thought, probably the result of instant blood-pressure rise. I didn't recognize "eat the Word," although I imagined he was saying something about the Bible, and about me consuming what was in it.

I've since learned to what he was referring – not a bland, fast-food diet, but fire-in-the-belly, spicy fare, down-home cooking; no sugared French fries, but meat and potatoes au gratin... and a taste of sweetness which frequently became bitter in the stomach.

I've enjoyed eating at your Table, Master: no high-fat, high-carb, low-energy meals in your kitchen! No cardboard propaganda painted to look like the Bread of Life. No wine-colored Kool-Aid pretending to be the life-blood of Jesus. Your Bread and Life may not always go down easy, but it will never fail to be choice, mouth-watering and energizing. Frequently, in my belly, anyway, it has burned. Here's to you, Lord! Here's gratitude. Long live God!

PSALM ONE-HUNDRED NINETEEN
"...awe at your words..."
(verses 161-168)

Jesus, when the story of the "great banquet" in Dr. Luke's Gospel began to open as a sunflower in my head, I was ecstatic; I got hooked on Luke. Not only was it thrilling; it calmed my soul. I'd long thought there was more to "the Good Samaritan" than "go and do likewise." That was good. There was more – lots more. It's impossible to plough the depths of "the Prodigal Sons." This greatest of stories ever told marches on through the years and eras and eons. Thank you, Word of life!

There are a thousand reasons to praise the Lord; so great is the joy within me now, it borders on fear! To listen to God, to hear God stops man-made Christendom in its tracks, every manufactured religion, to boot. What the Lord says reaches deeper than men can go, higher than humankind can reach. Every moment of our lives the Lord condescends to us. We cannot comprehend it! God bends low to us **not** because we're searching, exploring or rummaging the universe, hunting for a worthy god. God the holy eternal, the I AM comes down, bows and offers, leans over, stoops because God is love. God's love always stoops. How else could God reach us? We may climb but our ladders are short. This, this is God's sovereignty: God is love!

The Lord gives. We receive. God gives. We receive. Jesus gives. It will always be. Lord gives. We receive. There's such magnificence in it and in you, Living Word and our hope is to "follow your directions" and "abide by your counsel."

PSALM ONE-HUNDRED TWENTY-ONE
"A promise forever kept"

You're amazing, Lord! Not only for *how* you love but *that* you love *us* at all – all the time. Jesus, reveal the truth: is this but another of my attempts to veil my own love shortfall? I can't see how you love the whole of humanity, perhaps, because I can't (or don't) love many of those right around me – and none of them as you love. You're amazing!

There's no moment when you quit, wash your hands, get tired, lose patience, or grow sick and tired of us and walk away. How could it be? We shake our heads, not with cynicism or nay saying, but in *awe*. Yes, how *could* it be, Lord of eternal love? We *can* rejoice and be glad!

Living is good not because we have it all, or most of what earth can provide but, because *you* have us all. Joy comes from the heart of God. Nothing else is our true strength or salvation. Our Guardian and Creator never walks away. God's eyes are on the earthworm and starling.

God will not leave us. That's the promise forever kept.

PSALM ONE-HUNDRED TWENTY-TWO
"What it means to be Israel"

We may have forgotten, Jesus – or worse, abandoned our beginnings as nations. It appears we've decided your original intent no longer applies.

In my country, although our early years were a mixed bag of promise and forfeiture, we were *made* from many parts, cultures, colors and creeds. We were *intended* for freedom and became a place where the enslavement of men helped us make an enslaved nation. Cities, *meant* to be safe havens for immigrants, set aside hopeless ghettoes, instead.

Churches, called out from the fallen world to be communities of God-worship, hospitality to all, and healing chose, however, to become exclusive and excluding.

Lord, your "tribes" are in fact the many faces of humankind. But we have transmogrified our-selves into madding crowds of warring gangs and thugs.

You love *us*. We love ourselves and little else. You created sons and daughters, brothers and sisters, but we've become distant cousins and distrusting aliens. We have forgotten what it means and implies to be Israeli, Korean, German, Irish and North American.

It's transparent, Prince of Peace: we are intended to *BE* your shalom, reconcilers, peacemakers, good-news bringers. Forgive us. Come to our aid.

PSALM ONE-HUNDRED TWENTY-FIVE
"Rock solid!"

God of grace and mercy, you cannot be shoved or moved or made to abandon your people. Yours is a Gibraltar-solid God-commitment to all whom you have chosen and are redeeming.

"Those who trust in God are like Zion Mountain," *not* because *they* are rock solid, but because God is, and God holds *them* up and together. God's arms make them strong. The followers of Jesus do not gather around God, God gathers (around) and encircles them.

Only you know who among your children are gifted with hearts that are right, Lord. There are violent men, wicked men, and they whose hearts are wrong. Some may be ungrateful backsliders, rude, conceited, arrogant men whose hearts are far from God.

Lord, *you* know your own and those not your own in this world. Let there be in this and all the hearts of folk who love you the quest to be kind to, to care for and serve each and every living soul with whom our souls connect. Yes. Oh, yes!

PSALM ONE-HUNDRED TWENTY-SEVEN
"A Heart of Love"

Happy is the one in whom you create a heart of love, O Lord! Happy the church who celebrates the love songs of God in the midst of the congregation! Delighted are the souls who, in the face even of 'train wrecks,' remain steadfast because of "good fortune" – they are called children of God! Hear us, Lord! This happiness, this blessedness cannot be reproduced by the works of men; it's the free gift of the Father!

Abba, there's nothing like a happy church, or a soul who knows whom to praise! Praise **God**, all you gladsome saints! Blessed is the man, or woman who lives in awe before God, who cannot believe the "good fortune" the Lord has wrought. Give glory to the Great Creator! Such a man and woman rejoice and their church fills with the laughter of the family of God together. They sing exhilarated "Hallelujahs!" to God the Savior. Thank you, Lord of hosts!

A happy church or man rejoices in the mystery of God, in the wondrous mercies of God, in the goodness of the Eternal. A joyful woman or church over flows with praise to God – especially when trials come. We will not allow our thanksgivings to be sung merely in our times of prosperity.

A child, or church of God going through rough seasons does not falter in discouragement, but gives God adoring worship in every circumstance, and celebrates; there's no place to be but on God's side. This is our pledge, dear Lord.

There are moments and times, Lord, when people and churches will be grief stricken; times when, facing spiritual drought, a 'spirit' of gloom may overtake God's Body of Christ. These are the times, Lord, when your light needs to shine brightly, that men and women may once again be illumined. Thanks, praise, glory and honor belong to the living God! Amen.

PSALM ONE-HUNDRED TWENTY-EIGHT
"Your lush household"

Lord God, in which universe was this poet living? What world did this pilgrim inhabit? In what time and place? Which glorious generation was he serenading? Having lived in eight of these United States (four of them part the nation's *Bible Belt*), if such an idyllic place, household, or world exists, it hasn't revealed itself to me.

I'm *acquainted* with a few *individuals* who remind me somewhat of the spirit of the psalmist's words. I'd go further to say these folk remind me of qualities I see in Jesus – the "Jesus" I've visualized from reading the Gospels, anyway. I've known a few couples who, with their children, are amazing *models*, insofar as one man can ever know anyone else. In every instance, Lord, their lives are neither ideal nor comfortable… anything but!

One has cerebral palsy, one was divorced after long heartache; a couple lost their teenaged daughter to cancer; another couple watched their two-year-old slowly die of leukemia, had three late-term miscarriages and remains childless. Every one of them is a hero of mine. I'd say they've deserved much better than they've got.

I've seen and been with them, Lord, and not *one* of them is angry, or embittered, or in despair. All are humble and kind, thoughtful toward those in need, generous in giving themselves and everything they possess. I'm not *saying* they don't hurt and know the long pain of loss; that I don't know.

When I'm around them I always take heart. When they speak I always listen. As I live and breathe, they live the goodness of God, give themselves for the benefit of the suffering and walk the uneven, rocky road as *though* it is smooth and straight. I often thank the Lord for them.

PSALM ONE-HUNDRED THIRTY
"The bottom has fallen out..."

What's a person or church to do, Lord, when "the bottom" falls out? Do you hear our plea for help? How long, Lord, will your ears be shut to our "cries for mercy"? Why are we left hanging, O God? Are we on your gracious-ministrations schedule, or not?

Is it punishment for sins, Lord? Is this the reason you delay? We confess: if you were to *keep* score of our evils done or kindnesses still undone, we'd have no chance at all...*ever*. But the Word says you've a habit of forgiving. We ask it of you. We can do no else but thank you.

Are we, then, to conclude it's not our *sins* that have shut your ears and eyes to our pleadings? Is your *felt* absence *real*, or are our minds playing the devil's tricks on us? Do we simply need to heed your hesitation and wait?

If this spiritual sense of your scarcity, Jesus, is in reality your determination to wait until we develop *patience*, Father, to *wait* on the you for as long as it takes, and to be *satisfied* waiting – if that's your *decision*, Master – we will wait, secure in the knowledge you are with us in our waiting.

It's a sure thing: waiting on the Lord – in quiet and silence – in time becomes pregnant with God, and is nothing if not fervent, exciting, or in-structive. Boredom may greet us at the gate, only to be replaced by love and a quickened heart somewhere along the Way.

We will wait and watch and be alert, God. Your coming is love; your love is always on time. You are never too early, never too late. Come soon!

PSALM ONE-HUNDRED THIRTY-ONE
"Waiting"

In old age, Lord, keep me from imagining once upon a time I was a better person than I am now, or doing greater things than I do today. Teach me how to live creatively in real time now rather than to pass the hours away, dreaming of days gone by. Focus me on your hope for the wide world, not on my petty past accomplishment. Show me still the dissimilarity between wanting it all and having enough. Hold me on the right side of the fine line between personal arrogance and high confidence in you. Give me to know and live with quiet heart, instead of big head. Put these feet solidly on the ground of true wisdom, removing from them any hint of conceit or rudeness. Prevent me "trying to rule the roost" and bend me toward "serving the least of these." My need, Lord, is not to think fanciful thoughts, but to live your fruitful plans on behalf of others. Instruct me to these ends by your Word, Lord, that I may seek your mind and walk in your light.

PSALM ONE-HUNDRED THIRTY-THREE
"Outsiders"

It's sometimes a hard pinch, Lord, getting along with people we *know* and *love*, much less with *strangers* and the *strange*. It's *far* tougher to unite minds and temperaments with those we don't even like. And it's intensely more difficult among folk with whom we vehemently disagree and oppose.

The only way I can be *united* with religious fundamentalists, political arch-conservatives and cultural hedonists, Abba, is to keep my mouth shut and my spirit far too open. Frankly, that's a distant cry from unity, isn't it? The instant I speak with religious bigots and political ultra-right-wingers, my spirit and mind start shutting down. I didn't say this is *good*. It's how I am. My heart freezes. My muscles tighten. If I didn't drift into boredom, I'd get angry and want to find a way to get even.

Worst of all, in the presence of religious hyper-arrogance, my spirit and emotion slide outside. I choose to be an *outsider*. *I* remove myself. I have nothing to say and want nothing to do with persons who make like they are the good people of Jesus, but who sound and look *to me* like they never knew Jesus at all; anyway, not the Jesus I've met in Luke, Matthew and Mark.

What's most conspicuous about this, Rabboni, is my stuck-ness, stuffiness and un-Jesus-likeness. Father, were I never to like or appreciate them, give me love that's much larger than I. Show me the ways my spirit is bigoted, mean and legalistic. Cleanse me, Lord.

PSALM ONE-HUNDRED THIRTY-FIVE
"I Get It!"

The gods are many, Lord; you are God of all gods. My child-made god was my daddy; and, as 135:18 says bluntly, "Those who make them and trust them become like them." I get it! As a young pastor, my idol was Pastor Carlyle Marney, who was a wonderful mentor to me; I will forever give God thanks for him. At thirty, I still had an immature sense of self, of personal direction and very little sure foundation holding my own life. So I latched onto Marney's life and example: his preaching style, theology, social perceptions, biblical convictions, sense of humor... except, I had little knowledge, nothing wise or dynamic to say, a largely agnostic theology. I was a biblical novitiate.

Jesus, it took fifteen years to settle my own 'voice' and to live according to my own perceptions and vision. Frankly, **now**, as an elder disciple of yours, there are strong and still-changing convictions living inside and questions continue to multiply and hook themselves to the present sureties of my heart. I trust, but nothing is settled except an on-going joy of knowing you love me and all creation.

God, Marney will be always my most-honored mentor who made the lasting and widest impact in my life. I give thanks to you for him.

Mostly, Lord, I became like my dad. He shaped my life perhaps more, it seems to me now, even than you. He was an outdoorsman, loved young people, was a outstanding athlete, a dedicated naturalist, an environmentalist and fisherman beyond his time. At once I feared and adored him, and wanted to be like him. I trusted him with my life and wellbeing and, to some extent both great and small, became like him.

Father God, I slowly became aware of limitations, even flaws in both Marney and Dad. But, both of them helped teach and shape me, as did the culture and world in which I lived, learned and grew up. I'm suggesting that I really do hear and get the truth of the psalmist's words: "Those who make (gods) and trust them become like them." I find in this a very exhilarating, encouraging and hopeful thing; it seems almost a "law of human nature."

PSALM ONE-HUNDRED THIRTY-SEVEN
"Wherever we are..."

Lord God, I pray for the long line of folk who've found themselves on rocks, weeping! There's never been such weeping as theirs! Crying their hearts out, their tears of loss spill over, even onto their children. They're God-trusters, but God has treated/is treating them like dirt! Bile and grimness fill their bellies; they vomit acid and pain. What can they do on the dark and stony banks of an alien world? Are they to have a celebration of God? They're drowning, for goodness' sake! What is there but to beat their breasts with sticks while stuck on this waste heap called 'Babylon'? What, but weep?

God – swarms of people believe and act like they're in such alien places today, mired deep, up to their armpits in worry, rage and fear, and it's too much for them; there's no comfort anywhere. Trapped by sadness, they will not be consoled, or cheered, or encouraged. They're broken and have given up, or perhaps, they are lashing out. Many of them are angry and they're looking for someone to hate! "Where, in this hell, is God?" they cry, or snarl!

Was it Jeremiah, Father, who said something like: 'Wherever you are, in whatever situation, or condition you find yourself, build houses and live in them; marry and have children; give your children to the children of others, that they may bring forth families in the world. Plant crops and eat their produce?' In other words, "Do something. Do the next thing." I wonder, Lord, does/will/can this make any sense to fearful people in an alien world? Can people be God's people wherever they are, come what may, wherever God plants them, in whatever circumstance they find themselves? It's a hard one!

Jeremiah will preach! But, it will not be easy sermon preparation, or an easy sermon to hear.

PSALM ONE-HUNDRED THIRTY-NINE
"You know my thoughts"

Lord, I sometimes have to talk to know what I'm thinking, but you know every thought I have before a word comes out. You know precisely what I'd like to say, even when I don't or can't say it. Sometimes the word inside me is scatter-shot; it comes spewing out, confusing me and others. You know what I want to say and, often, what I want to say appears to be what people hear. Thank you for speaking to and through this heart and mouth! Thank you for making this servant worthy in your sight.

On occasion, I say good and right things, Lord, but you know how my heart churns and I worry. That's what bothers me. I forget that sermons are not for me or the church, but for you. I forget you can make a silk purse out of a sow's ear. I keep wanting and praying to preach better, but my sermons stay about the same. The problem is NOT with God's Word or God's Spirit. I've figured out where the problem is.

You, Lord, are pure light and your love illumines every hiding place; it always does. Too glorious to take in, you give yourself away, anyway. My words come through unclean lips, Jesus, from unclean breath, unclean heart and mind. Thank you! Thank you for your long-term cleaning-me-up process, for the sake of the Word and your Movement among us. So let be it!

PSALM ONE-HUNDRED THIRTY-NINE
"You shaped me"

I came out all right, Lord. Ten fingers, ten toes, one nose in the approximate middle of my face. It is amazing how often babies are born complete. I read how, when you formed Adam, you made Mud and slapped it together, breathed into the Mud's nostrils you'd made and Mud became a living nephesh. Then you took a rib out of Adam (was it before you breathed into Mud's nostrils?), bore it carefully into your private workshop, and, as Universal Artist, tenderly, lovingly molded the rib until it was Eve. Eve and Adam, too, were all together, strong and natural, bright and illumined inside.

Creator, you are astonishing and splendid! You made us, body and soul. You know every cell in us, every hair on us. You knew the parts we'd need and how exquisitely they'd function. Before our birth you set us breathing one amazing way; after we were birthed you used our kin to rouse and start us breathing a new way. How breathtaking and breath-giving you are! Sensational!

You spoke and whatever was, was? You knew us in the womb? You melded the parts and a billion cells into whole beings? We're miracles, but what else would we be, coming as we did from your hands? You're incredible! Lord, you're not rare; you're unique in the universe. We thank you, High God. You're unparalleled. You're marvelous; amazing is the Lord Eternal!

However, Lord, we don't understand why many of us come into this world whole, in our right minds, but many of us come broken – spina bifida, Downs syndrome, mental deficiencies and on and on. Medical explanations are devised by men for almost anything. But, why? Isn't this the **real** question? How did this happen? Why is an unborn slated to be a great pianist but another is bound, even as sperm meets ovum, to cerebral palsy?

There is no comfort to such insanity! Is there?

PSALM ONE-HUNDRED THIRTY-NINE
"whether I've done anything wrong"

Oh! My Lord! What **is** this? "Investigate my life, O God... See for yourself whether I've done anything wrong...!" Am I making a wrong assumption, understanding that the singer means, "I've done nothing wrong?"

Father, can you think of a way a saint would or could ever say this with a straight face? Without trembling? It's as if the poet is insinuating, "Look at me, Lord, take a good long look and see if there is any wicked way in me. Investigate my works; sift my deeds. Gaze with magnifying glass at both my exterior and interior. Look as long as you want. But... no matter how long or intensely you look, you'll find I've done nothing wrong. Ask all the questions you want, but the unalloyed picture you'll get is that I'm really okay. You're OK. I'm OK! Okay?"

Some one's way off base and out-of-line here, Father. Could or would a bona fide disciple of Jesus ever suggest, imply or dare say this? From where is this psalmist coming? Surely not from this world! How could a congregation muster the courage even to hum the tune, much less sing the song? Of course, it could be the phrasing of the translator. As for Jesus' people, however, it has to be, "Take me and lead me on the road to life eternal." Right!

PSALM ONE-HUNDRED THIRTY-NINE
"I can't get over you..."

Lord and God! I can't get past, around or beyond you. I can't get away from you. I know now: I can't go home without you, but I haven't yet been able to get used to you or comfortable with you. I can't get rid of you or get free of you to do my own thing. But I really don't want that, not much any more. I think, most of all, Lord, I can't get over you. Just can't get over you. You won't leave me alone or go from my mind for long. It's not a nuisance. Not now. I mostly welcome it now.

I even like to talk about you with others when they, also, want to talk. Honestly, it's they who usually start the conversation. I really would like to tell them how beautiful you are, and how wonderful. I would enjoy being able to sing beautifully and profoundly of your transcendent magnificence and mysterious revelations. I'm truly happy there are many who are able, who, by their ability to sing or speak of you so well, convince others you are nearer to us than air and more loving than we can imagine.

There's very little more that I can say, or have to say at the moment, so I'll say no more.

PSALM ONE-HUNDRED FORTY-ONE
"God, come close"

Yes, Lord, we are great pretenders, crying "Lord!" here, seeking "Lord!" there. Far from you, we maintain religious charades, raising unholy hands, shedding impious tears – play-acting, imagining you'll ignore our real indifference; thinking our self-righteousness is of no concern to you. We are miles from your beautiful presence. But you are ever near. Help us, Lord. "God, come close. Come quickly!"

We need day- and night-time guards at our mouths, Jesus, and watchmen 24/7 at our lips. Many times ours are dark thoughts in the night. Protect us from evil scheming. When we're in bad company, keep us from joining up. Make us yours, Father, so that our neighbors may see you in us. Prompt us to give you praise and thanksgiving. You can change bad apples to good, brilliant Lord, and make bad eggs into holy men.

Lord, bend us toward you until any wrong twists in us become tall and straight and useful. Thank you for being stronger than our pretensions, mightier than our self-deceptions and able to remake us into the likeness of Jesus. You are Lord!

PSALM ONE-HUNDRED FORTY-THREE
"A delicate, unsteady, breakable tribe"

The whole tenor of the psalm, Lord God, is how brittle we are, how tenuous our existence. We picture ourselves as resilient. We'll bend, but not break. We'll bloom in the desert if you water us. We don't require ubiquitous care, but the occasional "sound of your... voice" will suffice.

David nails another side of us, Father. We're not always sure... of self or life. We are sometimes vulnerable, unsteady and off-balance. What's the old saw? "Just because I'm paranoid doesn't mean they aren't talking about me." We will not shatter with every item of calamitous bad news, but if there's enough turmoil piling up day after day, we start to feel brittle and shop-worn.

We suspect that, from our beginning, human beings have lived perennially in crisis-mode, whether real or conjured. We're a tribe who need reassurance atop assurance. The song pleads, "Listen... pay attention... answer me... do what's right... hurry... don't turn away... wake me... point out... save me... teach me... lead me... keep up your reputation... give me life... get me out... vanquish my enemies... make a clean sweep..." In short, we're independent, but desperate for connection! Desperate for the Lord! If we get enough of your care, God, we'll "go to sleep each night trusting in you."

We're complex composites of capable plus insecure, confident and vacillating, steady-as-she-goes and walking-on-eggshells. We're bulls and butterflies, social dolphins and great white sharks, lions and lambs, mountain men and dainty lasses. We're the lost wanting to be found, pretending we've never been lost. We're children of God's light, plodding hours at a time in self-made dark. We're people of sundry gods, knowingly and subconsciously hungry for GOD. We're folk of amazing strength needing to cultivate the love that, to the strong, may seem weak, but is the mightiest power on earth.

The only sure thing we can think to say right now, Lord, is: you are the Lord; we are your children.

.

PSALM ONE-HUNDRED FORTY-FOUR
"...my mountain..."

Greater, higher are you, Abba, than the highest star and deeper than the depths of every sea. In you, we are safe; we cannot sink or drown – your bedrock love never stops; your works of wonder will be celebrated forever. We are God-blessed because you bend down to us, live in us and trust us with the bounty of your grace. You hold us up, and dear. We are sustained in the loving arms of Jesus.

We shall not stray or fall away; your voice will keep us oriented. You never get so fed up with us that you give us the boot. At times – maybe more times than we want to think – the demons see us a vast cloud of mite dust floating in the sun. To them we are nothing. They hate us. But, God, that is not you, not what you see. You see your children still trying, still praying, yielding to your voice, continuing in your love. Lord, please keep doing what you're doing...always.

We wonder often why we matter to you, Lord. Even our confidence in you and your mercy get shaky lots of times. We die and become dust again, Father. "We're like shadows (around) a campfire." We know you love us; we just can't figure out why.

PSALM ONE-HUNDRED FORTY-FIVE
"It is the truth"

It's the truth and nothing but the truth: "Everything God does is right – the trademark on all his works is love." It's the truth and nothing but: God does what God promises... always! God makes no disclaimers, has no small print or hidden agendas. God doesn't renege, default, recant, reverse or repudiate what God has said. God never over-states, re-phrases, back-pedals, reverses or cops out of God's word of hope and blessing.

We can count on it. "God sticks by all who love (God)... God's there, listening for all who pray... and mean it... God is gracious in everything (God) does." With the Lord, there's never, "I guess so" or "if I'm not busy" or "more or less" or "if there's time enough" or "I'll try."

We equivocate; the Lord does not. We shift and straddle; you stand firm. Even if we deny you, your love sticks like water to soil, penetrating the soul. If we die, because you live, we, also, shall be made alive, resurrected to new and unending life with you.

We will say, "Thank you, God!" but only your Holy Spirit can thank you for us enough!

PSALM ONE-HUNDRED FORTY-SIX
"Don't put your life in the hands of experts..."

Lord, the experts are sometimes dead wrong. The *experts expertly* announced, piously defended and unequivocally described their *expert* reasons why this, this, this and this university basketball team *should positively, unquestionably and finally* be ranked first in its north, south, east and west division in the March Madness round-ball tournament. Oops! Not one number one remains! A team ranked tenth, and another ranked eleventh have made it to final four. You probably know this all ready, Lord. I'm just talkin'.

Father, I'm not suggesting that your children don't need coaches, prognosticators, doctors, attorneys, teachers... – not at all!

It's *you* who know *all* there is to know about *life*, Savior, including "*salvation* life".

It's here I get a bit sideways about myself, Abba, and other *Really* religious sorts: preachers, Christian educators, ordained priests, popes, religion profs, the cloistered, philosophers of religion and the like. We "mere humans don't have what it takes" to be *real* expert. There is one whose name is *Jesus*.

The Master Expert never changes his mind because He is always right. "Zion's God *is* God for good!" Strange as it may seem in our *expert* ears: *God* "defends the wronged... feeds the hungry... frees prisoners... gives sight to the blind... lifts up the fallen... loves good people... protects strangers... takes the side of orphans and widows... but makes short work of the wicked."

I say "*strange*," Lord, because few if any of us *experts* would list these as ***our*** priorities in what's most important to our lives and living.

PSALM ONE-HUNDRED FORTY-SEVEN
"What matters?"

What else matters if we don't praise you, Lord? Thanking and praising you is no small part of our humanity. If we forget thanksgiving, everything else goes cockeyed and crazy. Without your praise living doesn't *fit*, life sours and we become withered-up shells acting out lines we do not know.

To speak the words, *thank you* and *we love you, Lord*, reminds us who our owner is, calls us to keener attention, puts *you* at *center*, activates the heart and calls us on to the Jesus-road.

We will praise you not because our praise is beautiful, but because *you* are. We will thank God for love not only because to do so is appropriate, but because God is the giver.

Without God's salvation-joy, living is a jigsaw puzzle with all the straight and corner pieces gone or missing. **Praising** you, Savior, puts all the pieces together again. Praising you makes us human. Rejoicing in Christ keeps us grounded and gives us wings.

What else *is* there if we do not praise and honor God's name?

PSALM ONE-HUNDRED FORTY-EIGHT
"No accumulation of praises…"

What word, poem or song could I pen, Holy Spirit, to express the acclamation you deserve? Would applause, plaudits, veneration, exaltation adequately sing it?

Nothing, Lord – no ode, lyric, verse or rhapsody – would come close!

Our devotion, our personal sacrifice in the name of your love seems in my mind little more than prattle, blather and drivel.

Abba God, I thank you for accepting as gold whatever is within and comes from me that's true praise and humble service. I'm amazed, Lord, that you accept what is only *partially* true of praise and servant-hood in me. It is awesome how you eternally consider the *source* of human praise and works.

I don't *want* to pretend but, many are the times I'm part real and part fake. I don't want to be a faker, Father, but you know me; when I'm *not* faking it on the outside, even then, some inner part of me may be. I don't need to be made better, with a tinker here and an adjustment there. Your work of creating me anew will never be done.

Thank you, Jesus, my Savior; I know your labor in me is the labor of your love to birth a child of heaven… while, up to this present moment, I continue to kick, squirm, object and dig in my rebel heels. I'd really appreciate if you would work on that in me, as well.

PSALM ONE-HUNDRED FORTY-NINE
"Sing to God a brand-new song…"

We don't have the words to "a brand-new song," Lord. But the urgency to sing it lives deep within. But the failure of *words* is not as much our weakness as your excellence. Our hearts are so full that any words are impotent to sing the loveliness of our God. We can but gawk and stare and gape at your creation. How wonderful is the Lord our God! We're thunderstruck by the thought of your power to re-create! Nothing can articulate the astonishment that stirs inside. You cherish us! Amen. AMEN!

PSALM ONE-HUNDRED FIFTY
"Praise"
(a bidding prayer)

We praise you for this house made holy by your love, O Lord…

We praise you for your creation and for making all things good…

We praise you, Lord, who gives us joy eternal and molds our hearts to be forever yours…

We praise you, Spirit of Christ, who walks beside us through the day and watches over us through the night…

We praise Jesus, the fragrance of life, the redolence of light, the salve, the balm of Gilead…

We praise Father, Son and Holy Spirit for God's music through the universe, tuning and turning our spirits to hear the generous song of Christ's peace…

We praise you, who love the children of earth and who plant a deep hunger in our souls to serve and worship God both today and always…

Lord, we thirst for you, we burn and pant for you, we covet you, the beautiful and lovely God, the Father of Jesus, Sovereign and Savior of humankind. God's people wait upon you in silence. We will bless, praise, worship and serve you, O Lord, now and eternally.

Lord, we are God's people who now thank you and, together, we say, "Amen!"

Paintings

*B*eing one of two children in an active family, our family of four always had wonderful story times together – dad told stories of the railroad, of having been a CCC man, playing baseball, going a semester to Wake Forest University, hunting, loving the outdoors and camping, of scouting and being a naturalist. Mom spoke of her growing up on a farm and of her sisters and half-brother.

As dad and son, the two of us invested ourselves widely in nature, played a lot as I grew and matured, learned to work and share together. He taught me to recognize trees and their leaves, to fish and hunt. Our conversations were often long and detailed.

While being far from a perfect family, we were usually free to speak, to agree and disagree, only rarely to be disagreeable and that not for long. We learned to see beauty wherever, to accept life's ups and downs, to enjoy events small and large. It was an open environment for me that allowed and encouraged adventure, working together, shared thoughtfulness and ideas. At the same time, I had a dad who unflinchingly called for high levels of personal commitment to things that healthy living involved.

Artistically, however, it was not until my early thirties, living in upstate New York, that I experienced an inveterate urge to express some of what seemed to reside inside me: that was, in visual, artistic form. So there began a quest in me to put some of my inner visions and thoughts in the shape of pencil/pen drawings, water paints, acrylics, oils, or mixed media. As years passed, discovering the necessity to parse time wisely, painting occurred between the times; artistic expression happened consistently, while my dominating personal thoughts, more often, occupied me as a teacher and clergyperson.

As you will see, the result of my artistic inclinations is revealed in rather homespun images, some of which are more representational, while a few come closer to impressionism. While I am not, by any stretch, offering the paintings as "high art," I hope you enjoy and find the renditions reminiscent of some of your own memories and inner imaginings from your own mind.

-Lee Anglin

Mountain Mama
Oil on canvas board

The Old Burr Oak
Oil on canvas board

Harbor Seekers
Acrylic on canvas board

The Vase
Oil and metallic on canvas

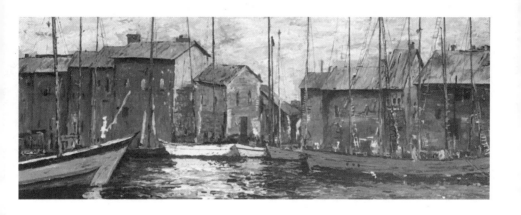

Portugal Portside
Acrylic on masonite

Cedar Peninsula
Oil on canvas board

Morning Mist
Ink and oil on canvas

The Bucket
Oil on canvas

Night Fisherman
Oil on driftwood

Rydal Water
Oil on canvas board

Favorite Spot
Oil on canvas board